THE WORKS OF
FRANCIS THOMPSON
POEMS: VOLUME II

Francis Thompson
Drawn by the Hon. Neville Lytton 1907

THE WORKS OF
FRANCIS THOMPSON
POEMS: VOLUME II

LONDON
BURNS OATES & WASHBOURNE LTD.

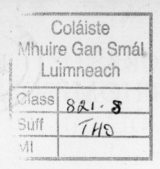
Twentieth Thousand

Made and Printed in Great Britain

THE CONTENTS

CONTENTS

CONTENTS

DEDICATION OF *NEW POEMS*

(1897)

To Coventry Patmore

LO, my book thinks to look Time's leaguer down,
  Under the banner of your spread renown !
  Or if these levies of impuissant rhyme
Fall to the overthrow of assaulting Time,
Yet this one page shall fend oblivious shame,
Armed with your crested and prevailing Name.

This dedication was written while the dear friend and great Poet to whom it was addressed yet lived. It is left as he saw it—the last verses of mine that were to pass under his eyes.

NOTES

THE ODE TO THE ENGLISH MARTYRS:
Some three hundred in all, of whom one hundred suffered at Tyburn; the first, John Houghton, Carthusian,
(4th May 1535); the last, Archbishop Oliver Plunket
(1st July 1681). Their names, including More and
Fisher, were added to the Roman Martyrology in
1886. To Ralph Sherwin and John Sugar are set
down the sayings quoted on page 135.

THE VICTORIAN ODE: The 'holy Poets' who
had died during the latter part of Queen Victoria's reign
were Tennyson, Browning, Matthew Arnold, Elizabeth Barrett Browning, Christina Rossetti, Dante
Gabriel Rossetti and Coventry Patmore.

*The Notes in the Text are the Poet's own, except where
they are enclosed in brackets.*

W. M.

SIGHT AND INSIGHT

*Wisdom is easily seen by them that love her, and is found by
them that seek her.*

To think therefore upon her is perfect understanding.

WISDOM, **vi.**

4

THE MISTRESS OF VISION

I

SECRET was the garden;
  Set i' the pathless awe
  Where no star its breath can draw.
Life, that is its warden,
Sits behind the fosse of death. Mine eyes saw not, and I
  saw.

II

It was a mazeful wonder;
  Thrice three times it was enwalled
  With an emerald—
Sealèd so asunder.
All its birds in middle air hung a-dream, their music
  thralled.

III

The Lady of fair weeping,
  At the garden's core,
  Sang a song of sweet and sore
And the after-sleeping;
In the land of Luthany, and the tracts of Elenore.

IV

With sweet-pangèd singing,
  Sang she through a dream-night's day;
  That the bowers might stay,
Birds bate their winging,
Nor the wall of emerald float in wreathèd haze away.

V

The lily kept its gleaming,
In her tears (divine conservers !)
Washèd with sad art ;
And the flowers of dreaming
Palèd not their fervours,
For her blood flowed through their nervures;
And the roses were most red, for she dipt them in her
heart.

VI

There was never moon,
Save the white sufficing woman :
Light most heavenly-human—
Like the unseen form of sound,
Sensed invisibly in tune,—
With a sun-derivèd stole
Did inaureole
All her lovely body round ;
Lovelily her lucid body with that light was interstrewn.

VII

The sun which lit that garden wholly,
Low and vibrant visible,
Tempered glory woke ;
And it seemèd solely
Like a silver thurible
Solemnly swung, slowly,
Fuming clouds of golden fire, for a cloud of incense-
smoke.

4

VIII

But woe 's me, and woe 's me,
For the secrets of her eyes !
In my visions fearfully
They are ever shown to be
As fringèd pools, whereof each lies
Pallid-dark beneath the skies
Of a night that is
But one blear necropolis.
And her eyes a little tremble, in the wind of her own
    sighs.

IX

Many changes rise on
Their phantasmal mysteries.
They grow to an horizon
Where earth and heaven meet ;
And like a wing that dies on
The vague twilight-verges,
Many a sinking dream doth fleet
Lessening down their secrecies.
And, as dusk with day converges,
Their orbs are troublously
Over-gloomed and over-glowed with hope and fear
    of things to be.

X

There is a peak on Himalay,
And on the peak undeluged snow,
And on the snow not eagles stray ;
There if your strong feet could go,—
Looking over tow'rd Cathay

5

From the never-deluged snow—
Farthest ken might not survey
Where the peoples underground dwell whom antique
    fables know.

XI

East, ah, east of Himalay,
Dwell the nations underground;
Hiding from the shock of Day,
For the sun's uprising-sound:
Dare not issue from the ground
At the tumults of the Day,
So fearfully the sun doth sound
Clanging up beyond Cathay;
For the great earthquaking sunrise rolling up beyond
    Cathay.

XII

Lend me, O lend me
The terrors of that sound,
That its music may attend me,
Wrap my chant in thunders round;
While I tell the ancient secrets in that Lady's singing
    found.

XIII

On Ararat there grew a vine;
When Asia from her bathing rose,
Our first sailor made a twine
Thereof for his prefiguring brows.
Canst divine
Where, upon our dusty earth, of that vine a cluster
    grows?

THE MISTRESS OF VISION

XIV

On Golgotha there grew a thorn
Round the long-prefigured Brows.
Mourn, O mourn!
For the vine have we the spine? Is this all the Heaven
allows?

XV

On Calvary was shook a spear;
Press the point into thy heart—
Joy and fear!
All the spines upon the thorn into curling tendrils start.

XVI

O dismay!
I, a wingless mortal, sporting
With the tresses of the sun?
I, that dare my hand to lay
On the thunder in its snorting?
Ere begun,
Falls my singed song down the sky, even the old Icarian
way.

XVII

From the fall precipitant
These dim snatches of her chant
Only have remainèd mine;—
That from spear and thorn alone
May be grown
For the front of saint or singer any divinizing twine.

7

XVIII

Her song said that no springing
Paradise but evermore
Hangeth on a singing
That has chords of weeping,
And that sings the after-sleeping
To souls which wake too sore.
'But woe the singer, woe!' she said; 'beyond the dead
    his singing-lore,
    All its art of sweet and sore,
    He learns, in Elenore!'

XIX

Where is the land of Luthany,
Where is the tract of Elenore?
I am bound therefor.

XX

'Pierce thy heart to find the key;
With thee take
Only what none else would keep;
Learn to dream when thou dost wake,
Learn to wake when thou dost sleep;
Learn to water joy with tears,
Learn from fears to vanquish fears,
To hope, for thou dar'st not despair,
Exult, for that thou dar'st not grieve;
Plough thou the rock until it bear;
Know, for thou else couldst not believe;
Lose, that the lost thou may'st receive;
Die, for none other way canst live.

8

When earth and heaven lay down their veil,
And that apocalypse turns thee pale ;
When thy seeing blindeth thee
To what thy fellow-mortals see ;
When their sight to thee is sightless ;
Their living, death ; their light, most lightless ;
Search no more—
Pass the gates of Luthany, tread the region Elenore.'

XXI

Where is the land of Luthany,
And where the region Elenore ?
I do faint therefor.

XXII

' When to the new eyes of thee
All things by immortal power,
Near or far,
Hiddenly
To each other linkèd are,
That thou canst not stir a flower
Without troubling of a star ;
When thy song is shield and mirror
To the fair snake-curlèd Pain,
Where thou dar'st affront her terror
That on her thou may'st attain
Perséan conquest ; seek no more,
O seek no more !
Pass the gates of Luthany, tread the region Elenore.'

9

XXIII

So sang she, so wept she,
Through a dream-night's day ;
And with her magic singing kept she—
Mystical in music—
That garden of enchanting
In visionary May ;
Swayless for my spirit's haunting,
Thrice-threefold walled with emerald from our mortal
mornings grey.

XXIV

And as a necromancer
Raises from the rose-ash
The ghost of the rose ;
My heart so made answer
To her voice's silver plash,—
Stirred in reddening flash,
And from out its mortal ruins the purpureal phantom
blows.

XXV

Her tears made dulcet fretting,
Her voice had no word,
More than thunder or the bird.
Yet, unforgetting,
The ravished soul her meanings knew. Mine ears
heard not, and I heard.

THE MISTRESS OF VISION

XXVI

When she shall unwind
All those wiles she wound about me,
Tears shall break from out me,
That I cannot find
Music in the holy poets to my wistful want, I doubt me!

CONTEMPLATION

THIS morning saw I, fled the shower,
The earth reclining in a lull of power:
The heavens, pursuing not their path,
Lay stretched out naked after bath,
Or so it seemed; field, water, tree, were still,
Nor was there any purpose on the calm-browed hill.

The hill, which sometimes visibly is
Wrought with unresting energies,
Looked idly; from the musing wood,
And every rock, a life renewed
Exhaled like an unconscious thought
When poets, dreaming unperplexed,
Dream that they dream of nought.
Nature one hour appears a thing unsexed,
Or to such serene balance brought
That her twin natures cease their sweet alarms,
And sleep in one another's arms.
The sun with resting pulses seems to brood,
And slacken its command upon my unurged blood.

The river has not any care
Its passionless water to the sea to bear;
The leaves have brown content;
The wall to me has freshness like a scent,
And takes half-animate the air,
Making one life with its green moss and stain;
And life with all things seems too perfect blent
For anything of life to be aware.
The very shades on hill, and tree, and plain,

CONTEMPLATION

Where they have fallen doze, and where they
    doze remain.

No hill can idler be than I ;
No stone its inter-particled vibration
Investeth with a stiller lie ;
No heaven with a more urgent rest betrays
The eyes that on it gaze.
We are too near akin that thou shouldst cheat
Me, Nature, with thy fair deceit.
In poets floating like a water-flower
Upon the bosom of the glassy hour,
In skies that no man sees to move,
Lurk untumultuous vortices of power,
For joy too native, and for agitation
Too instant, too entire for sense thereof,
Motion like gnats when autumn suns are low,
Perpetual as the prisoned feet of love
On the heart's floors with painèd pace that go.
From stones and poets you may know,
Nothing so active is, as that which least seems so.

For he, that conduit running wine of song,
Then to himself does most belong
When he his mortal house unbars
To the importunate and thronging feet
That round our corporal walls unheeded beat ;
Till, all containing, he exalt
His stature to the stars, or stars
Narrow their heaven to his fleshly vault :
When, like a city under ocean,

SIGHT AND INSIGHT

To human things he grows a desolation,
And is made a habitation
For the fluctuous universe
To lave with unimpeded motion.
He scarcely frets the atmosphere
With breathing, and his body shares
The immobility of rocks ;
His heart's a drop-well of tranquillity ;
His mind more still is than the limbs of fear,
And yet its unperturbed velocity
The spirit of the simoom mocks.
He round the solemn centre of his soul
Wheels like a dervish, while his being is
Streamed with the set of the world's harmonies,
In the long draft of whatsoever sphere
He lists the sweet and clear
Clangour of his high orbit on to roll,
So gracious is his heavenly grace ;
And the bold stars does hear,
Every one in his airy soar,
For evermore
Shout to each other from the peaks of space,
As 'thwart ravines of azure shouts the mountaineer.

'BY REASON OF THY LAW'

HERE I make oath—
Although the heart that knows its
bitterness
Hear loath,
And credit less—
That he who kens to meet Pain's kisses fierce
Which hiss against his tears,
Dread, loss, nor love frustrate,
Nor all iniquity of the froward years
Shall his inurèd wing make idly bate,
Nor of the appointed quarry his staunch sight
To lose observance quite ;
Seal from half-sad and all-elate
Sagacious eyes
Ultimate Paradise ;
Nor shake his certitude of haughty fate.

Pacing the burning shares of many dooms,
I with stern tread do the clear-witting stars
To judgement cite,
If I have borne aright
The proving of their pure-willed ordeal.
From food of all delight
The heavenly Falconer my heart debars,
And tames with fearful glooms
The haggard to His call ;
Yet sometimes comes a hand, sometimes a
voice withal,
And she sits meek now, and expects the light.

SIGHT AND INSIGHT

In this Avernian sky,
This sultry and incumbent canopy
Of dull and doomed regret ;
Where on the unseen verges yet, O yet,
At intervals,
Trembles, and falls,
Faint lightning of remembered transient
  sweet—
Ah, far too sweet
But to be sweet a little, a little sweet, and
  fleet ;
Leaving this pallid trace,
This loitering and most fitful light, a space,
Still some sad space,
For Grief to see her own poor face :—
Here where I keep my stand
With all o'er-anguished feet,
And no live comfort near on any hand ;
Lo, I proclaim the unavoided term,
When this morass of tears, then drained
  and firm,
Shall be a land—
Unshaken I affirm—
Where seven-quired psalterings meet ;
And all the gods move with calm hand in
  hand,
And eyes that know not trouble and the
  worm.

THE DREAD OF HEIGHT

If ye were blind, ye should have no sin : but now ye say :
We see : your sin remaineth. JOHN ix. 41.

NOT the Circean wine
  Most perilous is for pain :
  Grapes of the heavens' star-loaden vine,
Whereto the lofty-placed
Thoughts of fair souls attain,
Tempt with a more retributive delight,
And do disrelish all life's sober taste.
'Tis to have drunk too well
The drink that is divine,
Maketh the kind earth waste,
And breath intolerable.

Ah me !
How shall my mouth content it with mortality ?
Lo, secret music, sweetest music,
From distances of distance drifting its lone
      flight,
Down the arcane where Night would perish
      in night,
Like a god's loosened locks slips undulously :
Music that is too grievous of the height
For safe and low delight,
Too infinite
For bounded hearts which yet would girth the
      sea !

SIGHT AND INSIGHT

So let it be,
Though sweet be great, and though my heart
    be small :
So let it be,
O music, music, though you wake in me
No joy, no joy at all ;
Although you only wake
Uttermost sadness, measure of delight,
Which else I could not credit to the height,
Did I not know,
That ill is statured to its opposite ;
Did I not know,
And even of sadness so,
Of utter sadness, make
Of extreme sad a rod to mete
The incredible excess of unsensed sweet,
And mystic wall of strange felicity.
So let it be,
Though sweet be great, and though my heart
    be small,
And bitter meat
The food of gods for men to eat ;
Yea, John ate daintier, and did tread
Less ways of heat,
Than whom to their wind-carpeted
High banquet-hall,
And golden love-feasts, the fair stars entreat.

But ah ! withal,
Some hold, some stay,
O difficult Joy, I pray,

THE DREAD OF HEIGHT

Some arms of thine,
Not only, only arms of mine !
Lest like a weary girl I fall
From clasping love so high,
And lacking thus thine arms, then may
Most hapless I
Turn utterly to love of basest rate ;
For low they fall whose fall is from the sky.
Yea, who me shall secure
But I, of height grown desperate,
Surcease my wing, and my lost fate
Be dashed from pure
To broken writhings in the shameful slime :
Lower than man, for I dreamed higher,
Thrust down, by how much I aspire,
And damned with drink of immortality ?
For such things be,
Yea, and the lowest reach of reeky Hell
Is but made possible
By foreta'en breath of Heaven's austerest clime.

These tidings from the vast to bring
Needeth not doctor nor divine,
Too well, too well
My flesh doth know the heart-perturbing thing ;
That dread theology alone
Is mine,
Most native and my own ;
And ever with victorious toil
When I have made
Of the deific peaks dim escalade,

SIGHT AND INSIGHT

My soul with anguish and recoil
Doth like a city in an earthquake rock,
As at my feet the abyss is cloven then,
With deeper menace than for other men,
Of my potential cousinship with mire ;
That all my conquered skies do grow a hollow mock,
My fearful powers retire,
No longer strong,
Reversing the shook banners of their song.

Ah, for a heart less native to high Heaven,
A hooded eye, for jesses and restraint,
Or for a will accipitrine to pursue !—
The veil of tutelar flesh to simple livers given,
Or those brave-fledging fervours of the Saint,
Whose heavenly falcon-craft doth never taint,
Nor they in sickest time their ample virtue mew.

ORIENT ODE

LO, in the sanctuaried East,
Day, a dedicated priest
In all his robes pontifical exprest,
Lifteth slowly, lifteth sweetly,
From out its Orient tabernacle drawn,
Yon orbèd sacrament confest
Which sprinkles benediction through the dawn ;
And when the grave procession 's ceased,
The earth with due illustrious rite
Blessed,—ere the frail fingers featly
Of twilight, violet-cassocked acolyte,
His sacerdotal stoles unvest—
Sets, for high close of the mysterious feast,
The sun in august exposition meetly
Within the flaming monstrance of the West.

O salutaris hostia,
Quæ cœli pandis ostium !
Through breachèd darkness' rampart, a
Divine assaulter, art thou come !
God whom none may live and mark !
Borne within thy radiant ark,
While the Earth, a joyous David,
Dances before thee from the dawn to dark.
The moon, O leave, pale ruined Eve ;
Behold her fair and greater daughter*
Offers to thee her fruitful water,
Which at thy first white *Ave* shall conceive !

* The earth.

SIGHT AND INSIGHT

Thy gazes do on simple her
Desirable allures confer ;
What happy comelinesses rise
Beneath thy beautifying eyes !
Who was, indeed, at first a maid
Such as, with sighs, misgives she is not fair,
And secret views herself afraid,
Till flatteries sweet provoke the charms they swear ;
Yea, thy gazes, blissful Lover,
Make the beauties they discover !
What dainty guiles and treacheries caught
From artful prompting of love's artless
        thought
Her lowly loveliness teach her to adorn,
When thy plumes shiver against the conscious
        gates of morn !

And so the love which is thy dower,
Earth, though her first-frightened breast
Against the exigent boon protest
(For she, poor maid, of her own power
Has nothing in herself, not even love,
But an unwitting void thereof),
Gives back to thee in sanctities of flower ;
And holy odours do her bosom invest,
That sweeter grows for being prest :
Though dear recoil, the tremorous nurse of joy,
From thine embrace still startles coy,
Till Phosphor lead, at thy returning hour,
The laughing captive from the wishing West.

22

Nor the majestic heavens less
Thy formidable sweets approve,
Thy dreads and thy delights confess,
That do draw, and that remove.
Thou as a lion roar'st, O Sun,
Upon thy satellites' vexèd heels;
Before thy terrible hunt thy planets run;
Each in his frighted orbit wheels,
Each flies through inassuageable chase,
Since the hunt o' the world begun,
The puissant approaches of thy face,
And yet thy radiant leash he feels.
Since the hunt o' the world begun,
Lashed with terror, leashed with longing,
The mighty course is ever run;
Pricked with terror, leashed with longing,
Thy rein they love, and thy rebuke they shun.
Since the hunt o' the world began,
With love that trembleth, fear that loveth,
Thou join'st the woman to the man;
And Life with Death
In obscure nuptials moveth,
Commingling alien yet affinèd breath.

Thou art the incarnated Light
Whose Sire is aboriginal, and beyond
Death and resurgence of our day and night;
From him is thy vicegerent wand
With double potence of the black and white.
Giver of Love, and Beauty, and Desire,
The terror, and the loveliness, and purging,

The deathfulness and lifefulness of fire !
Samson's riddling meanings merging
In thy twofold sceptre meet :
Out of thy minatory might,
Burning Lion, burning Lion,
Comes the honey of all sweet,
And out of thee, the Eater, comes forth meat.
And though, by thine alternate breath,
Every kiss thou dost inspire
Echoeth
Back from the windy vaultages of death ;
Yet thy clear warranty above
Augurs the wings of death too must
Occult reverberations stir of love
Crescent, and life incredible ;
That even the kisses of the just
Go down not unresurgent to the dust.
Yea, not a kiss which I have given,
But shall triumph upon my lips in heaven,
Or cling a shameful fungus there in hell.

Know'st thou me not, O Sun ? Yea, well
Thou know'st the ancient miracle,
The children know'st of Zeus and May ;
And still thou teachest them, O splendent
    Brother,
To incarnate, the antique way,
The truth which is their heritage from their Sire
In sweet disguise of flesh from their sweet
    Mother.
My fingers thou hast taught to con

ORIENT ODE

Thy flame-chorded psalterion,
Till I can translate into mortal wire—
Till I can translate passing well—
The heavenly harping harmony,
Melodious, sealed, inaudible,
Which makes the dulcet psalter of the world's
    desire.
Thou whisperest in the Moon's white ear,
And she does whisper into mine,—
By night together, I and she—
With her virgin voice divine,
The things I cannot half so sweetly tell
As she can sweetly speak, I sweetly hear.

By her, the Woman, does Earth live, O Lord,
Yet she for Earth, and both in Thee.
Light out of Light!
Resplendent and prevailing Word
Of the Unheard!
Not unto thee, great Image, not to thee
Did the wise heathen bend an idle knee;
And in an age of faith grown frore
If I too shall adore,
Be it accounted unto me
A bright sciential idolatry!
God has given thee visible thunders
To utter thine apocalypse of wonders;
And what want I of prophecy,
That at the sounding from thy station
Of thy flagrant trumpet, see
The seals that melt, the open revelation ?

Or who a God-persuading angel needs,
That only heeds
The rhetoric of thy burning deeds ?
Which but to sing, if it may be,
In worship-warranting moiety,
So I would win
In such a song as hath within
A smouldering core of mystery,
Brimmèd with nimbler meanings up
Than hasty Gideons in their hands may sup ;—
Lo, my suit pleads
That thou, Isaian coal of fire,
Touch from yon altar my poor mouth's desire,
And the relucent song take for thy sacred meeds.

To thine own shape
Thou round'st the chrysolite of the grape,
Bind'st thy gold lightnings in his veins ;
Thou storest the white garners of the rains.
Destroyer and preserver, thou
Who medicinest sickness, and to health
Art the unthankèd marrow of its wealth ;
To those apparent sovereignties we bow
And bright appurtenances of thy brow !
Thy proper blood dost thou not give,
That Earth, the gusty Mænad, drink and dance ?
Art thou not life of them that live ?
Yea, in glad twinkling advent, thou dost dwell
Within our body as a tabernacle !
Thou bittest with thine ordinance
The jaws of Time, and thou dost mete

ORIENT ODE

The unsustainable treading of his feet.
Thou to thy spousal universe
Art Husband, she thy Wife and Church;
Who in most dusk and vidual curch,
Her Lord being hence,
Keeps her cold sorrows by thy hearse.
The heavens renew their innocence
And morning state
But by thy sacrament communicate;
Their weeping night the symbol of our prayers,
Our darkened search,
And sinful vigil desolate.
Yea, biune in imploring dumb,
Essential Heavens and corporal Earth await;
The Spirit and the Bride say: Come!
Lo, of thy Magians I the least
Haste with my gold, my incenses and myrrhs,
To thy desired epiphany, from the spiced
Regions and odorous of Song's traded East.
Thou, for the life of all that live
The victim daily born and sacrificed;
To whom the pinion of this longing verse
Beats but with fire which first thyself didst give,
To thee, O Sun—or is't perchance to Christ?

Ay, if men say that on all high heaven's face
The saintly signs I trace
Which round my stolèd altars hold their solemn
        place,
Amen, amen! For oh, how could it be,—
When I with wingèd feet had run

Through all the windy earth about,
Quested its secret of the sun,
And heard what thing the stars together shout,—
I should not heed thereout
Consenting counsel won :—
' By this, O Singer, know we if thou see.
When men shall say to thee : Lo ! Christ is here,
When men shall say to thee : Lo ! Christ is there,
Believe them : yea, and this—then art thou seer,
When all thy crying clear
Is but : Lo here ! lo there !—ah me, lo everywhere ! '

NEW YEAR'S CHIMES

WHAT is the song the stars sing ?
 (*And a million songs are as song of one*)
 This is the song the stars sing :
(*Sweeter song's none*)

One to set, and many to sing,
 (*And a million songs are as song of one*)
One to stand, and many to cling,
The many things, and the one Thing,
 The one that runs not, the many that run.

The ever new weaveth the ever old,
 (*And a million songs are as song of one*)
Ever telling the never told ;
The silver saith, and the said is gold,
 And done ever the never done.

The Chase that's chased is the Lord o' the chase,
 (*And a million songs are as song of one*)
And the Pursued cries on the race ;
 And the hounds in leash are the hounds that
 run.

Hidden stars by the shown stars' sheen ;
 (*And a million suns are but as one*)
Colours unseen by the colours seen,
And sounds unheard heard sounds between,
 And a night is in the light of the sun.

SIGHT AND INSIGHT

An ambuscade of light in night,
  (*And a million secrets are but as one*)
And a night is dark in the sun's light,
  And a world in the world man looks upon.

Hidden stars by the shown stars' wings,
  (*And a million cycles are but as one*)
And a world with unapparent strings
Knits the simulant world of things ;
  Behold, and vision thereof is none.

The world above in the world below,
  (*And a million worlds are but as one*)
And the One in all ; as the sun's strength so
Strives in all strength, glows in all glow
  Of the earth that wits not, and man thereon.

Braced in its own fourfold embrace
  (*And a million strengths are as strength of one*)
And round it all God's arms of grace,
The world, so as the Vision says,
  Doth with great lightning-tramples run.

And thunder bruiteth into thunder,
  (*And a million sounds are as sound of one*)
From stellate peak to peak is tossed a voice of
    wonder,
And the height stoops down to the depths there-
    under,
  And sun leans forth to his brother-sun.

NEW YEAR'S CHIMES

And the more ample years unfold
  (*With a million songs as song of one*)
A little new of the ever old,
A little told of the never told,
  Added act of the never done.

Loud the descant, and low the theme,
  (*A million songs are as song of one*)
And the dream of the world is dream in dream,
But the one Is is, or nought could seem ;
  And the song runs round to the song begun.

This is the song the stars sing,
  (*Tonèd all in time*)
Tintinnabulous, tuned to ring
A multitudinous-single thing
  (*Rung all in rhyme*).

FROM THE NIGHT OF FOREBEING

AN ODE AFTER EASTER

In the chaos of preordination, and night of our forebeings.
                                    SIR THOMAS BROWNE.

Et lux in tenebris erat, et tenebræ eam non comprehende-
runt.   ST. JOHN.

CAST wide the folding doorways of the East,
    For now is light increased !
    And the wind-besomed chambers of the air,
See they be garnished fair ;
And look the ways exhale some precious odours,
And set ye all about wild-breathing spice,
Most fit for Paradise !
Now is no time for sober gravity,
Season enough has Nature to be wise ;
But now discinct, with raiment glittering free,
Shake she the ringing rafters of the skies
With festal footing and bold joyance sweet,
And let the earth be drunken and carouse !
For lo, into her house
Spring is come home with her world-wandering feet,
And all things are made young with young desires ;
And all for her is light increased
In yellow stars and yellow daffodils,
And East to West, and West to East,
Fling answering welcome-fires,
By dawn and day-fall, on the jocund hills.
And ye, winged minstrels of her fair meinie,

FROM THE NIGHT OF FOREBEING

Being newly coated in glad livery,
Upon her steps attend,
And round her treading dance, and without end
Reel your shrill lutany.
What popular breath her coming does out-tell
The garrulous leaves among!
What little noises stir and pass
From blade to blade along the voluble grass!
O Nature, never-done
Ungaped-at Pentecostal miracle,
We hear thee, each man in his proper tongue!
Break, elemental children, break ye loose
From the strict frosty rule
Of grey-beard Winter's school.
Vault, O young winds, vault in your tricksome courses
Upon the snowy steeds that reinless use
In cœrule pampas of the heaven to run;
Foaled of the white sea-horses,
Washed in the lambent waters of the sun.
Let even the slug-abed snail upon the thorn
Put forth a conscious horn!
Mine elemental co-mates, joy each one;
And ah, my foster-brethren, seem not sad—
No, seem not sad,
That my strange heart and I should be so little glad.
Suffer me at your leafy feast
To sit apart, a somewhat alien guest,
And watch your mirth,
Unsharing in the liberal laugh of earth;
Yet with a sympathy
Begot of wholly sad and half-sweet memory—

SIGHT AND INSIGHT

The little sweetness making grief complete ;
Faint wind of wings from hours that distant beat,
When I, I too,
Was once, O wild companions, as are you,—
Ran with such wilful feet ;
Wraith of a recent day and dead,
Risen wanly overhead,
Frail, strengthless as a noon-belated moon,
Or as the glazing eyes of watery heaven,
When the sick night sinks into deathly swoon.

A higher and a solemn voice
I heard through your gay-hearted noise ;
A solemn meaning and a stiller voice
Sounds to me from far days when I too shall rejoice,
Nor more be with your jollity at strife.
O prophecy
Of things that are, and are not, and shall be !
The great-vanned Angel March
Hath trumpeted
His clangorous ' Sleep no more ' to all the dead—
Beat his strong vans o'er earth, and air, and sea.
And they have heard ;
Hark to the *Jubilate* of the bird
For them that found the dying way to life !
And they have heard,
And quicken to the great precursive word ;
Green spray showers lightly down the cascade of
    the larch ;
The graves are riven,

FROM THE NIGHT OF FOREBEING

And the Sun comes with power amid the clouds
    of heaven !
Before his way
Went forth the trumpet of the March ;
Before his way, before his way
Dances the pennon of the May !
O Earth, unchilded, widowed Earth, so long
Lifting in patient pine and ivy-tree
Mournful belief and steadfast prophecy,
Behold how all things are made true !
Behold your bridegroom cometh in to you,
Exceeding glad and strong.
Raise up your eyes, O raise your eyes abroad !
No more shall you sit sole and vidual,
Searching, in servile pall,
Upon the hieratic night the star-sealed sense of all :
Rejoice, O barren, and look forth abroad !
Your children gathered back to your embrace
See with a mother's face ;
Look up, O mortals, and the portent heed !
In very deed,
Washed with new fire to their irradiant birth,
Reintegrated are the heavens and earth ;
From sky to sod,
The world's unfolded blossom smells of God.

O imagery
Of that which was the first, and is the last !
For, as the dark profound nativity,
God saw the end should be,
When the world's infant horoscope He cast.

Unshackled from the bright Phœbean awe,
In leaf, flower, mold, and tree,
Resolved into dividual liberty,
Most strengthless, unparticipant, inane,
Or suffered the ill peace of lethargy,
Lo, the Earth eased of rule :
Unsummered, granted to her own worst smart
The dear wish of the fool—
Disintegration, merely which man's heart
For freedom understands,
Amid the frog-like errors from the damp
And quaking swamp
Of the low popular levels spawned in all the lands.
But thou, O Earth, dost much disdain
The bondage of thy waste and futile reign,
And sweetly to the great compulsion draw
Of God's alone true-manumitting law,
And Freedom, only which the wise intend,
To work thine innate end.
Over thy vacant counterfeit of death
Broods with soft urgent breath
Love, that is child of Beauty and of Awe :
To intercleavage of sharp warring pain,
As of contending chaos come again,
Thou wak'st, O Earth,
And work'st from change to change and birth to
      birth
Creation old as hope, and new as sight ;
For meed of toil not vain,
Hearing once more the primal fiat toll :
' Let there be light ! '

FROM THE NIGHT OF FOREBEING

And there is light !
Light flagrant, manifest,
Light to the zenith, light from pole to pole,
Light from the East that waxeth to the West,
And with its puissant goings-forth
Encroaches on the South and on the North ;
And with its great approaches does prevail
Upon the sullen fastness of the height,
And summoning its levied power
Crescent and confident through the crescent hour,
Goes down with laughters on the subject vale :
Light flagrant, manifest,
Light to the sentient closeness of the breast,
Light to the secret chambers of the brain !
And thou up-floatest, warm, and newly-bathed,
Earth, through delicious air,
And with thine own apparent beauties swathed,
Wringing the waters from thine arborous hair ;
That all men's hearts, which do behold and see,
Grow weak with their exceeding much desire,
And turn to thee on fire,
Enamoured with their utter wish of thee,
Anadyomene !
What vine-outquickening life all creatures sup,
Feel, for the air within its sapphire cup
How it does leap, and twinkle headily !
Feel, for Earth's bosom pants, and heaves her scarf-
ing sea ;
And round and round in bacchanal rout reel the
swift spheres intemperably !

SIGHT AND INSIGHT

My little-worlded self! the shadows pass
In this thy sister-world, as in a glass,
Of all processions that revolve in thee:
Not only of cyclic Man
Thou here discern'st the plan,
Not only of cyclic Man, but of the cyclic Me.
Not solely of Mortality's great years
The reflex just appears,
But thine own bosom's year, still circling round
In ample and in ampler gyre
Toward the far completion, wherewith crowned
Love unconsumed shall chant in his own furnace-fire.
How many trampled and deciduous joys
Enrich thy soul for joys deciduous still,
Before the distance shall fulfil
Cyclic unrest with solemn equipoise!
Happiness is the shadow of things past,
Which fools still take for that which is to be!
And not all foolishly:
For all the past, read true, is prophecy,
And all the firsts are hauntings of some Last,
And all the springs are flash-lights of one Spring.
Then leaf, and flower, and fall-less fruit
Shall hang together on the unyellowing bough;
And silence shall be Music mute
For her surchargèd heart. Hush thou!
These things are far too sure that thou should'st dream
Thereof, lest they appear as things that seem.

Shade within shade! for deeper in the glass
Now other imaged meanings pass;

FROM THE NIGHT OF FOREBEING

And as the man, the poet there is read.
Winter with me, alack !
Winter on every hand I find :
Soul, brain, and pulses dead,
The mind no further by the warm sense fed,
The soul weak-stirring in the arid mind,
More tearless-weak to flash itself abroad
Than the earth's life beneath the frost-scorched sod.
My lips have drought, and crack,
By laving music long unvisited.
Beneath the austere and macerating rime
Draws back constricted in its icy urns
The genial flame of Earth, and there
With torment and with tension does prepare
The lush disclosures of the vernal time.
All joys draw inward to their icy urns,
Tormented by constraining rime,
And there
With undelight and throe prepare
The bounteous efflux of the vernal time.
Nor less beneath compulsive Law
Rebukèd draw
The numbèd musics back upon my heart ;
Whose yet-triumphant course I know
And prevalent pulses forth shall start,
Like cataracts that with thunderous hoof charge the
    disbanding snow.
All power is bound
In quickening refusal so ;
And silence is the lair of sound ;
In act its impulse to deliver,

SIGHT AND INSIGHT

With fluctuance and quiver
The endeavouring thew grows rigid. Strong
From its retracted coil strikes the resilient song.

Giver of spring,
And song, and every young new thing!
Thou only seest in me, so stripped and bare,
The lyric secret waiting to be born,
The patient term allowed
Before it stretch and flutteringly unfold
Its rumpled webs of amethyst-freaked, diaphanous gold.
And what hard task abstracts me from delight,
Filling with hopeless hope and dear despair
The still-born day and parchèd fields of night,
That my old way of song, no longer fair,
For lack of serene care,
Is grown a stony and a weed-choked plot,
Thou only know'st aright,
Thou only know'st, for I know not.
How many songs must die that this may live!
And shall this most rash hope and fugitive,
Fulfilled with beauty and with might
In days whose feet are rumorous on the air,
Make me forget to grieve
For songs which might have been, nor ever were?
Stern the denial, the travail slow,
The struggling wall will scantly grow:
And though with that dread rite of sacrifice
Ordained for during edifice,
How long, how long ago!
Into that wall which will not thrive

FROM THE NIGHT OF FOREBEING

I build myself alive,
Ah, who shall tell me will the wall uprise ?
Thou wilt not tell me, who dost only know !
Yet still in mind I keep,
He that observes the wind shall hardly sow,
He that regards the clouds shall hardly reap.
Thine ancient way ! I give,
Nor wit if I receive ;
Risk all, who all would gain : and blindly. Be it so.

' And blindly,' said I ?—No !
That saying I unsay : the wings
Hear I not in prævenient winnowings
Of coming songs, that lift my hair and stir it ?
What winds with music wet do the sweet storm
      foreshow !
Utter stagnation
Is the solstitial slumber of the spirit,
The blear and blank negation of all life :
But these sharp questionings mean strife, and strife
Is the negation of negation.
The thing from which I turn my troubled look,
Fearing the gods' rebuke ;
That perturbation putting glory on,
As is the golden vortex in the West
Over the foundered sun ;
That—but low breathe it, lest the Nemesis
Unchild me, vaunting this—
Is bliss, the hid, hugged, swaddled bliss !
O youngling Joy carest !
That on my now first-mothered breast

Pliest the strange wonder of thine infant lip,
What this aghast surprise of keenest panging,
Wherefrom I blench, and cry thy soft mouth rest ?
Ah hold, withhold, and let the sweet mouth slip !
So, with such pain, recoils the woolly dam,
Unused, affrighted, from her yeanling lamb :
I, one with her in cruel fellowship,
Marvel what unmaternal thing I am.

Nature, enough ! Within thy glass
Too many and too stern the shadows pass.
In this delighted season, flaming
For thy resurrection-feast,
Ah, more I think the long ensepulture cold,
Than stony winter rolled
From the unsealed mouth of the holy East ;
The snowdrop's saintly stoles less heed
Than the snow-cloistered penance of the seed.
'Tis the weak flesh reclaiming
Against the ordinance
Which yet for just the accepting spirit scans.
Earth waits, and patient heaven,
Self-bonded God doth wait
Thrice-promulgated bans
Of His fair nuptial-date.
And power is man's,
With that great word of ' Wait,'
To still the sea of tears,
And shake the iron heart of Fate.
In that one word is strong
An else, alas, much-mortal song ;

FROM THE NIGHT OF FOREBEING

With sight to pass the frontier of all spheres,
And voice which does my sight such wrong.

Not without fortitude I wait
The dark majestical ensuit
Of destiny, nor peevish rate
Calm-knowledged Fate.
I, that no part have in the time's bragged way,
And its loud bruit ;
I, in this house so rifted, marred,
So ill to live in, hard to leave ;
I, so star-weary, over-warred,
That have no joy in this your day—
Rather foul fume englutting, that of day
Confounds all ray—
But only stand aside and grieve ;
I yet have sight beyond the smoke,
And kiss the gods' feet, though they wreak
Upon me stroke and again stroke ;
And this my seeing is not weak.
The Woman I behold, whose vision seek
All eyes and know not ; t'ward whom climb
The steps o' the world, and beats all wing of rhyme,
And knows not ; 'twixt the sun and moon
Her inexpressible front enstarred
Tempers the wrangling spheres to tune ;
Their divergent harmonies
Concluded in the concord of her eyes,
And vestal dances of her glad regard.
I see, which fretteth with surmise
Much heads grown unsagacious-grey,

SIGHT AND INSIGHT

The slow aim of wise-hearted Time,
Which folded cycles within cycles cloak :
We pass, we pass, we pass ; this does not pass away,
But holds the furrowing earth still harnessed to its yoke.
The stars still write their golden purposes
On heaven's high palimpsest, and no man sees,
Nor any therein Daniel ; I do hear
From the revolving year
A voice which cries :
' All dies ;
Lo, how all dies ! O seer,
And all things too arise :
All dies, and all is born ;
But each resurgent morn, behold, more near the Perfect
    Morn.'

Firm is the man, and set beyond the cast
Of Fortune's game, and the iniquitous hour,
Whose falcon soul sits fast,
And not intends her high sagacious tour
Or ere the quarry sighted ; who looks past
To slow much sweet from little instant sour,
And in the first does always see the last.

ANY SAINT

HIS shoulder did I hold
Too high that I, o'erbold
    Weak one,
Should lean thereon.

But He a little hath
Declined His stately path
    And my
Feet set more high;

That the slack arm may reach
His shoulder, and faint speech
    Stir
His unwithering hair.

And bolder now and bolder
I lean upon that shoulder,
    So dear
He is and near:

And with His aureole
The tresses of my soul
    Are blent
In wished content.

Yea, this too gentle Lover
Hath flattering words to move her
    To pride
By His sweet side.

SIGHT AND INSIGHT

Ah, Love ! somewhat let be—
Lest my humility
Grow weak
When Thou dost speak.

Rebate Thy tender suit,
Lest to herself impute
Some worth
Thy bride of earth !

A maid too easily
Conceits herself to be
Those things
Her lover sings ;

And being straitly wooed,
Believes herself the Good
And Fair
He seeks in her.

Turn something of Thy look,
And fear me with rebuke,
That I
May timorously

Take tremors in Thy arms,
And with contrivèd charms
Allure
A love unsure.

Not to me, not to me,
Builded so flawfully,
O God,
Thy humbling laud !

ANY SAINT

Not to this man, but Man,—
Universe in a span;
      Point
   Of the spheres conjoint;

In whom eternally
Thou, Light, dost focus Thee!—
     Didst pave
   The way o' the wave;

Rivet with stars the Heaven,
For causeways to Thy driven
      Car
   In its coming far

Unto him, only him;
In Thy deific whim
     Didst bound
   Thy works' great round

In this small ring of flesh;
The sky's gold-knotted mesh
     Thy wrist
   Did only twist

To take him in that net.—
Man! swinging-wicket set
     Between
   The Unseen and Seen;

Lo, God's two worlds immense,
Of spirit and of sense,
     Wed
   In this narrow bed;

SIGHT AND INSIGHT

Yea, and the midge's hymn
Answers the seraphim
      Athwart
       Thy body's court !

Great arm-fellow of God !
To the ancestral clod
      Kin,
       And to cherubin ;

Bread predilectedly
O' the worm and Deity !
      Hark,
       O God's clay-sealed Ark,

To praise that fits thee, clear
To the ear within the ear,
      But dense
       To clay-sealed sense.

All the Omnific made
When, in a word he said,
      (Mystery !)
       He uttered *thee* ;

Thee His great utterance bore,
O secret metaphor
      Of what
       Thou dream'st no jot !

Cosmic metonymy ;
Weak world-unshuttering key ;
      One
       Seal of Solomon !

ANY SAINT

Trope that itself not scans
Its huge significance,
      Which tries
    Cherubic eyes !

Primer where the angels all
God's grammar spell in small,
      Nor spell
    The highest too well !

Point for the great descants
Of starry disputants ;
      Equation
    Of creation !

Thou meaning, couldst thou see,
Of all which dafteth thee ;
      So plain,
    It mocks thy pain.

Stone of the Law indeed,
Thine own self couldst thou read ;
      Thy bliss
    Within thee is.

Compost of Heaven and mire,
Slow foot and swift desire !
      Lo,
    To have Yes, choose No ;

Gird, and thou shalt unbind ;
Seek not, and thou shalt find ;
      To eat,
    Deny thy meat ;

SIGHT AND INSIGHT

And thou shalt be fulfilled
With all sweet things unwilled :
    So best
    God loves to jest

With children small—a freak
Of heavenly hide-and-seek
    Fit
    For thy wayward wit,

Who art thyself a thing
Of whim and wavering ;
    Free
    When His wings pen thee ;

Sole fully blest, to feel
God whistle thee at heel ;
    Drunk up
    As a dew-drop,

When He bends down, sun-wise,
Intemperable eyes ;
    Most proud,
    When utterly bowed,

To feel thyself and be
His dear nonentity—
    Caught
    Beyond human thought

In the thunder-spout of Him,
Until thy being dim,
    And be
    Dead deathlessly.

ANY SAINT

Stoop, stoop ; for thou dost fear
The nettle's wrathful spear,
    So slight
    Art thou of might !

Rise ; for Heaven hath no frown
When thou to thee pluck'st down,
    Strong clod !
    The neck of God.

ASSUMPTA MARIA

Thou needst not make new songs, but say the old.—COWLEY.

'MORTALS, that behold a Woman
      Rising 'twixt the Moon and Sun ;
      Who am I the heavens assume ? an
All am I, and I am one.

' Multitudinous ascend I,
    Dreadful as a battle arrayed,
For I bear you whither tend I ;
    Ye are I : be undismayed !
I, the Ark that for the graven
    Tables of the Law was made ;
Man's own heart was one ; one, Heaven ;
    Both within my womb were laid.
      For there Anteros with Eros,
        Heaven with man, conjoinèd was,—
      Twin-stone of the Law, *Ischyros,*
        Agios Athanatos.

' I, the flesh-girt Paradises
    Gardenered by the Adam new,
Daintied o'er with dear devices
    Which He loveth, for He grew.
I, the boundless strict Savannah
    Which God's leaping feet go through ;
I, the Heaven whence the Manna,
    Weary Israel, slid on you !

ASSUMPTA MARIA

He the Anteros and Eros,
   I the body, He the Cross ;
He upbeareth me, *Ischyros*,
   Agios Athanatos !

' I am Daniel's mystic Mountain,
   Whence the mighty stone was rolled ;
I am the four Rivers' Fountain,
   Watering Paradise of old ;
Cloud down-raining the Just One am,
   Danae of the Shower of Gold ;
I the Hostel of the Sun am ;
   He the Lamb, and I the Fold.
   He the Anteros and Eros,
      I the body, He the Cross ;
   He is fast to me, *Ischyros*,
      Agios Athanatos !

' I, the Presence-hall where Angels
   Do enwheel their placèd King—
Even my thoughts which, without change else,
   Cyclic burn and cyclic sing.
To the hollow of Heaven transplanted,
   I a breathing Eden spring,
Where with venom all outpanted
   Lies the slimed Curse shrivelling.
   For the brazen Serpent clear on
      That old fangèd knowledge shone ;
   I to Wisdom rise, *Ischyron*,
      Agion Athanaton !

' Then commanded and spake to me
 He who framed all things that be ;
And my Maker entered through me,
 In my tent His rest took He.
Lo ! He standeth, Spouse and Brother,
 I to Him, and He to me,
Who upraised me where my mother
 Fell, beneath the apple-tree.
  Risen 'twixt Anteros and Eros,
   Blood and Water, Moon and Sun,
  He upbears me, He *Ischyros*,
   I bear Him, the *Athanaton !* '

Where is laid the Lord arisen ?
 In the light we walk in gloom ;
Though the Sun has burst his prison,
 We know not his biding-room.
Tell us where the Lord sojourneth,
 For we find an empty tomb.
' Whence He sprung, there he returneth,
 Mystic Sun,—the Virgin's Womb.'
  Hidden Sun, His beams so near us,
   Cloud-enpillared as He was
  From of old, there He, *Ischyros*,
   Waits our search, *Athanatos*.

Who is She, in candid vesture,
 Rushing up from out the brine ?
Treading with resilient gesture
 Air, and with that Cup divine ?

54

ASSUMPTA MARIA

She in us and we in her are,
  Beating Godward : all that pine,
Lo, a wonder and a terror—
  The Sun hath blushed the Sea to Wine !
  He the Anteros and Eros,
    She the Bride and Spirit ; for
  Now the days of promise near us,
    And the Sea shall be no more.

Open wide thy gates, O Virgin,
  That the King may enter thee !
At all gates the clangours gurge in,
  God's paludament lightens, see !
Camp of Angels ! Well we even
  Of this thing may doubtful be,—
If thou art assumed to Heaven,
  Or is Heaven assumed to thee !
    Consummatum. Christ the promised,
      Thy maiden realm, is won, O Strong !
    Since to such sweet Kingdom comest,
      Remember me, poor Thief of Song !

Cadent fails the stars along :—
  Mortals, that behold a woman
    Rising 'txixt the Moon and Sun ;
  Who am I the heavens assume ? an
    All am I, and I am one.

55

CARMEN GENESIS

I

SING how the uncreated Light
    Moved first upon the deep and night,
    And, at Its *fiat lux*,
Created light unfurled, to be
God's pinions—stirred perpetually
    In flux and in reflux.

From light create, and the vexed ooze,
God shaped to potency and thews
    All things we see, and all
Which lessen, beyond human mark,
Into the spaces Man calls dark
    Because his day is small.

Far-storied, lanterned with the skies,
All Nature, magic-palace-wise,
    Did from the waters come :
The angelic singing-masons knew
How many centuried centuries through
    The awful courses clomb.

The regent light his strong decree
Then laid upon the snarling sea ;
    Shook all its wallowing girth
The shaggy brute, and did (for wrath
Low bellowing in its chafèd path)
    Sullen disglut the Earth.

CARMEN GENESIS

Meanwhile the universal light
Broke itself into bounds ; and Night
   And Day were two, yet one :
Dividual splendour did begin
Its procreant task, and, globing, spin
   In moon, and stars, and sun.

With interspheral counterdance
Consenting contraries advance,
   And plan is hid for plan :
In roaring harmonies would burst
The thunder's throat; the heavens, uncurst,
   Restlessly steady ran.

All day Earth waded in the sun,
Free-bosomed ; and, when Night begun,
   Spelt in the secret stars.
Day unto Day did utter speech,
Night unto Night the knowledge teach
   Barred in its golden bars.

And, last, Man's self, the little world
Where was Creation's semblance furled,
   Rose at the linking nod :
For the first world, the moon and sun
Swung orbed. That human second one
   Was dark, and waited God.

His locks He spread upon the breeze,
His feet He lifted on the seas,
   Into His worlds He came :

SIGHT AND INSIGHT

Man made confession : ' There is Light ! '
And named, while Nature to its height
   Quailed, the enormous Name.

II

Poet ! still, still thou dost rehearse,
In the great *fiat* of thy Verse,
   Creation's primal plot ;
And what thy Maker in the whole
Worked, little maker, in thy soul
   Thou work'st, and men know not.

Thine intellect, a luminous voice,
Compulsive moved above the noise
   Of thy still-fluctuous sense ;
And Song, a water-child like Earth,
Stands with feet sea-washed, a wild birth
   Amid their subsidence.

Bold copyist ! who dost relimn
The traits, in man's gross mind grown dim,
   Of the first Masterpiece—
Re-marking all in thy one Day :—
God give thee Sabbath to repay
   Thy sad work with full peace !

Still Nature, to the clang of doom,
Thy Verse rebeareth in her womb ;
   Thou makest all things new,
Elias, when thou comest ! yea,
Mak'st straight the intelligential way
   For God to pace into.

His locks perturb man's eddying thought,
His feet man's surgy breast have sought,
   To man, His World, He came ;
Man makes confession : ' There is Light ! '
And names, while Being to its height
   Rocks, the desirèd Name.

III

God ! if not yet the royal siege
Of Thee, my terrible sweet Liege,
   Hath shook my soul to fall ;
If, 'gainst Thy great investment, still
Some broken bands of rebel Will
   Do man the desperate wall ;

Yet, yet, Thy graciousness ! I tread,
All quick, through tribes of moving dead—
   Whose life's a sepulchre
Sealed with the dull stone of a heart
No angel can roll round. I start,
   Thy secrets lie so bare !

With beautiful importunacy
All things plead, ' We are fair ! ' To me
   Thy world's a morning haunt,
A bride whose zone no man hath slipt
But I, with baptism still bedript
   Of the prime water's font.

AD CASTITATEM

THROUGH thee, Virginity, endure
The stars, most integral and pure,
    And ever contemplate
    Themselves inviolate

In waters, and do love unknown
Beauty they dream not is their own !
    Through thee the waters bare
    Their bosoms to the air,

And with confession never done
Admit the sacerdotal sun,
    Absolved eternally
    By his asperging eye.

To tread the floor of lofty souls,
With thee Love mingles aureoles ;
    Who walk his mountain-peak
    Thy sister-hand must seek.

A hymen all unguessed of men
In dreams thou givest to my ken ;
    For lacking of like mate,
    Eternally frustrate :

Where, that the soul of either spouse
Securelier clasp in either's house,
    They never breach at all
    Their walls corporeal.

AD CASTITATEM

This was the secret of the great
And primal Paradisal state,
  Which Adam and which Eve
  Might not again retrieve.

Yet hast thou toward my vision taught
A way to draw in vernal thought,
  Not all too far from that
  Great Paradisal state,

Which for that earthy men might wrong,
Were 't uttered in this earthless song,
  Thou layest cold finger-tips
  Upon my histed lips.

But thou, who knowest the hidden thing
Thou hast instructed me to sing,
  Teach Love the way to be
  A new Virginity !

Do thou with thy protecting hand
Shelter the flame thy breath has fanned ;
  Let my heart's reddest glow
  Be but as sun-flushed snow.

And if they say that snow is cold,
O Chastity, must they be told
  The hand that 's chafed with snow
  Takes a redoubled glow ?—

SIGHT AND INSIGHT

That extreme cold like heat doth sear ?
O to this heart of love draw near,
 And feel how scorching rise
 Its white-cold purities!

Life, ancient and o'er-childed nurse,
To turn my thirsting mouth averse,
 Her breast embittereth
 With wry foretaste of death:

But thou, sweet Lady Chastity,
Thou, and thy brother Love with thee,
 Upon her lap may'st still
 Sustain me, if thou will.

Out of the terrors of the tomb,
And unclean shapes that haunt sleep's gloom,
 Yet, yet I call on thee,—
 ' Abandon thou not me ! '

Now sung is all the singing of this chant.
Lord, Lord, be nigh unto me in my want !
For to the idols of the Gentiles I
Will never make me an hierophant :—
Their false-fair gods of gold and ivory,
Which have a mouth, nor any speech thereby,
Save such as soundeth from the throat of hell
The aboriginal lie ;
And eyes, nor any seeing in the light,—
Gods of the obscene night,
To whom the darkness is for diadem.

AD CASTITATEM

Let them that serve them be made like to them,
Yea, like to him who fell
Shattered in Gaza, as the Hebrews tell,
Before the simple presence of the Ark.

My singing is gone out upon the dark.

THE AFTER WOMAN

DAUGHTER of the ancient Eve,
We know the gifts ye gave—and give.
Who knows the gifts which *you* shall give,
Daughter of the newer Eve ?
You, if my soul be augur, you
Shall—O what shall you not, Sweet, do ?
The celestial traitress play,
And all mankind to bliss betray ;
With sacrosanct cajoleries
And starry treachery of your eyes,
Tempt us back to Paradise !
Make heavenly trespass ;—ay, press in
Where faint the fledge-foot seraphin,
Blest fool ! Be ensign of our wars,
And shame us all to warriors !
Unbanner your bright locks,—advance,
Girl, their gilded puissance
I' the mystic vaward, and draw on
After the lovely gonfalon
Us to out-folly the excess
Of your sweet foolhardiness ;
To adventure like intense
Assault against Omnipotence !

Give me song, as She is, new,
Earth should turn in time thereto !
New, and new, and thrice so new,
All old sweets, New Sweet, meant you !
Fair, I had a dream of thee,

THE AFTER WOMAN

When my young heart beat prophecy,
And in apparition elate
Thy little breasts knew waxèd great,
Sister of the Canticle,
And thee for God grown marriageable.

How my desire desired your day,
That, wheeled in rumour on its way,
Shook me thus with presentience ! Then
Eden's lopped tree shall shoot again :
For who Christ's eyes shall miss, with those
Eyes for evident nuncios ?
Or who be tardy to His call
In your accents augural ?
Who shall not feel the Heavens hid
Impend, at tremble of your lid,
And divine advent shine avowed
Under that dim and lucid cloud ;
Yea, 'fore the silver apocalypse,
Fail, at the unsealing of your lips ?
When to love *you* is (O Christ's Spouse !)
To love the beauty of His house ;
Then come the Isaian days ; the old
Shall dream ; and our young men behold
Vision—yea, the vision of Thabor-mount,
Which none to other shall recount,
Because in all men's hearts shall be
The seeing and the prophecy.
For ended is the Mystery Play,
When Christ is life, and you the way ;
When Egypt's spoils are Israel's right,

SIGHT AND INSIGHT

And Day fulfils the married arms of Night.
But here my lips are still.
Until
You and the hour shall be revealed,
This song is sung and sung not, and its words
    are sealed.

GRACE OF THE WAY

'MY brother!' spake she to the sun;
　　The kindred kisses of the stars
　　Were hers; her feet were set upon
The moon. If slumber solved the bars

Of sense, or sense transpicuous grown
　　Fulfillèd seeing unto sight,
I know not; nor if 'twas my own
　　Ingathered self that made her night.

The windy trammel of her dress,
　　Her blown locks, took my soul in mesh;
God's breath they spake, with visibleness
　　That stirred the raiment of her flesh:

And sensible, as her blown locks were,
　　Beyond the precincts of her form
I felt the woman flow from her—
　　A calm of intempestuous storm.

I failed against the affluent tide;
　　Out of this abject earth of me
I was translated and enskied
　　Into the heavenly-regioned She.

Now of that vision I bereaven
　　This knowledge keep, that may not dim:—
Short arm needs man to reach to Heaven,
　　So ready is Heaven to stoop to him;

SIGHT AND INSIGHT

Which sets, to measure of man's feet,
   No alien Tree for trysting-place ;
And who can read, may read the sweet
   Direction in his Lady's face.

And pass and pass the daily crowd,
   Unwares, occulted Paradise ;
Love the lost plot cries silver-loud,
   Nor any know the tongue he cries.

The light is in the darkness, and
   The darkness doth not comprehend :
God hath no haste ; and God's sons stand
   Yet a day, tarrying for the end.

Dishonoured Rahab still hath hid,
   Yea still, within her house of shame,
The messengers by Jesus bid
   Forerun the coming of His Name.

The Word was flesh, and crucified,
   From the beginning, and blasphemed :
Its profaned raiment men divide,
   Damned by what, reverenced, had redeemed.

Thy Lady, was thy heart not blind,
   One hour gave to thy witless trust
The key thou go'st about to find ;
   And thou hast dropped it in the dust.

GRACE OF THE WAY

Of her, the Way's one mortal grace,
  Own, save thy seeing be all forgot,
That, truly, God was in this place,
  And thou, unblessèd, knew'st it not.

But some have eyes, and will not see ;
  And some would see, and have not eyes ;
And fail the tryst, yet find the Tree,
  And take the lesson for the prize.

RETROSPECT

ALAS, and I have sung
    Much song of matters vain,
    And a heaven-sweetened tongue
Turned to unprofiting strain
Of vacant things, which though
Even so they be, and throughly so,
It is no boot at all for thee to know,
But babble and false pain.

What profit if the sun
Put forth his radiant thews,
And on his circuit run,
Even after my device, to this and to that use;
And the true Orient, Christ,
Make not His cloud of thee?
I have sung vanity,
And nothing well devised.

And though the cry of stars
Give tongue before His way
Goldenly, as I say,
And each from wide Saturnus to hot Mars
He calleth by its name,
Lest that its bright feet stray;
And thou have lore of all,
But to thine own Sun's call
Thy path disorbed hast never wit to tame;
It profits not withal,
And my rede is but lame.

RETROSPECT

Only that, 'mid vain vaunt
Of wisdom ignorant,
A little kiss upon the feet of Love
My hasty verse has stayed
Sometimes a space to plant ;
It has not wholly strayed,
Not wholly missed near sweet, fanning proud
    plumes above.

Therefore I do repent
That with religion vain,
And misconceivèd pain,
I have my music bent
To waste on bootless things its skiey-gendered
    rain :
Yet shall a wiser day
Fulfil more heavenly way
And with approvèd music clear this slip,
I trust in God most sweet.
Meantime the silent lip,
Meantime the climbing feet.

A NARROW VESSEL

BEING A LITTLE DRAMATIC SEQUENCE ON
THE ASPECT OF PRIMITIVE GIRL-NATURE
TOWARDS A LOVE BEYOND ITS CAPACITIES

A GIRL'S SIN

I.—IN HER EYES

CROSS child ! red, and frowning so ?
'I, the day just over,
Gave a lock of hair to—no !
How *dare* you say, my lover ? '

He asked you ?—Let me understand ;
Come, child, let me sound it !
'Of course, he *would* have asked it, and—
And so—somehow—he—found it.

'He told it out with great loud eyes—
Men have such little wit !
His sin I ever will chastise
Because I gave him it.

'Shameless in me the gift, alas !
In him his open bliss :
But for the privilege he has
A thousand he shall miss !

'His eyes, where once I dreadless laughed,
Call up a burning blot :
I hate him, for his shameful craft
That asked by asking not !'

75

A NARROW VESSEL

Luckless boy ! and all for hair
    He never asked, you said ?
' Not just—but then he gazed—I swear
    He gazed it from my head !

' His silence on my cheek like breath
    I felt in subtle way ;
More sweet than aught another saith
    Was what he did not say.

' He 'll think me vanquished, for this lapse,
    Who should be above him ;
Perhaps he 'll think me light ; perhaps—
    Perhaps he 'll think I—love him !

' Are his eyes conscious and elate,
    I hate him that I blush ;
Or are they innocent, still I hate—
    They mean a thing 's to hush.

' Before he naught amiss could do,
    Now all things show amiss ;
'Twas all my fault, I know that true,
    But all my fault was his.

' I hate him for his mute distress,
    'Tis insult he should care !
Because my heart 's all humbleness,
    All pride is in my air.

A GIRL'S SIN

' With him, each favour that I do
    Is bold suit's hallowing text ;
Each gift a bastion levelled to
    The next one and the next.

' Each wish whose grant may him befall
    Is clogged by those withstood ;
He trembles, hoping one means all,
    And I, lest perhaps it should.

' Behind me piecemeal gifts I cast,
    My fleeing self to save ;
And that 's the thing must go at last,
    For that 's the thing he 'd have.

' My lock the enforcèd steel did grate
    To cut ; its root-thrills came
Down to my bosom. It might sate
    His lust for my poor shame !

' His sifted dainty this should be
    For a score ambrosial years !
But his too much humility
    Alarums me with fears.

' My gracious grace a breach he counts
    For graceless escalade ;
And, though he 's silent ere he mounts,
    My watch is not betrayed.

77

A NARROW VESSEL

' My heart hides from my soul he 's sweet :
    Ah dread, if he divine !
One touch, I might fall at his feet,
    And he might rise from mine.

' To hear him praise my eyes' brown gleams
    Was native, safe delight ;
But now it usurpation seems,
    Because I've given him right.

' Before, I'd have him not remove ;
    Now, would not have him near ;
With sacrifice I called on Love,
    And the apparition's Fear.'

Foolish to give it !—' 'Twas my whim,
    When he might parted be,
To think that I should stay by him
    In a little piece of me.

' He always said my hair was soft—
    What touches he will steal !
Each touch and look (and he 'll look oft)
    I almost thought I'd feel.

' And then, when first he saw the hair,
    To think his dear amazement !
As if he wished from skies a star,
    And found it in his casement.

A GIRL'S SIN

' He 'd kiss the lock—and I had toyed
  With dreamed delight of this :
But ah, in proof, delight was void—
  I could not *see* his kiss ! '

So, fond one, half this agony
  Were spared, which my hand hushes,
Could you have played, Sweet, the sweet spy,
  And blushed not for your blushes !

A GIRL'S SIN

II.—IN HIS EYES

CAN I forget her cruelty
    Who, brown miracle, gave you me?
    Or with unmoisted eyes think on
The proud surrender overgone
(Lowlihead in haughty dress)
Of the tender tyranness?
And ere thou for my joy wast given,
How rough the road to that blest heaven!
With what pangs I fore-expiated
Thy cold outlawry from her head;
How was I trampled and brought low,
Because her virgin neck was so;
How thralled beneath the jealous state
She stood at point to abdicate;
How sacrificed, before to me
She sacrificed her pride and thee;
How did she, struggling to abase
Herself to do me strange, sweet grace,
Enforce unwitting me to share
Her throes and abjectness with her;
Thence heightening that hour when her lover
Her grace, with trembling, should discover,
And in adoring trouble be
Humbled at her humility!
And with what pitilessness was I
After slain, to pacify
The uneasy *manes* of her shame,

A GIRL'S SIN

Her haunting blushes!—Mine the blame:
What fair injustice did I rue
For what I—did not tempt her to!
Nor aught the judging maid might win
Me to assoil from *her* sweet sin.
But naught were extreme punishment
For that beyond-divine content,
When my with-thee-first-giddied eyes
Stooped ere their due on Paradise!
O hour of consternating bliss
When I heavened me in thy kiss;
Thy softness (daring overmuch!)
Profanèd with my licensed touch;
Worshipped, with tears, on happy knee,
Her doubt, her trust, her shyness free,
Her timorous audacity!

LOVE DECLARED

I LOOKED, she drooped, and neither spake, and
    cold
  We stood, how unlike all forecasted thought
Of that desirèd minute ! Then I leaned
Doubting ; whereat she lifted—oh, brave eyes
Unfrighted :—forward like a wind-blown flame
Came bosom and mouth to mine !
                    That falling kiss
Touching long-laid expectance, all went up
Suddenly into passion ; yea, the night
Caught, blazed, and wrapt us round in vibrant fire.

Time's beating wing subsided, and the winds
Caught up their breathing, and the world's great
    pulse
Stayed in mid-throb, and the wild train of life
Reeled by, and left us stranded on a hush.
This moment is a statue unto Love
Carved from a fair white silence.
                  Lo, he stands
Within us—are we not one now, one, one roof,
His roof, and the partition of weak flesh
Gone down before him, and no more for ever ?—
Stands like a bird new-lit, and as he lit,
Poised in our quiet being ; only, only
Within our shaken hearts the air of passion,
Cleft by his sudden coming, eddies still
And whirs round his enchanted movelessness.

LOVE DECLARED

A film of trance between two stirrings ! Lo,
It bursts ; yet dream's snapped links cling round the
    limbs
Of waking : like a running evening stream
Which no man hears, or sees, or knows to run,
(Glazed with dim quiet,) save that there the moon
Is shattered to a creamy flicker of flame,
Our eyes' sweet trouble were hid, save that the love
Trembles a little on their impassioned calms.

THE WAY OF A MAID

THE lover whose soul shaken is
   In some decuman billow of bliss,
   Who feels his gradual-wading feet
Sink in some sudden hollow of sweet,
And 'mid love's usèd converse comes
Sharp on a mood which all joy sums,
An instant's fine compendium of
The liberal-leavèd writ of love—
His abashed pulses beating thick
At the exigent joy and quick,
Is dumbed, by aiming utterance great
Up to the miracle of his fate.

The wise girl, such Icarian fall
Saved by her confidence that she's small,—
As what no kindred word will fit
Is uttered best by opposite,
Love in the tongue of hate exprest,
And deepest anguish in a jest,—
Feeling the infinite must be
Best said by triviality,
Speaks, where expression bates its wings,
Just happy, alien, little things ;
What of all words is in excess
Implies in a sweet nothingness ;
With dailiest babble shows her sense
That full speech were full impotence ;
And, while she feels the heavens lie bare,
She only talks about her hair.

BEGINNING OF END

SHE was aweary of the hovering
  Of Love's incessant and tumultuous wing;
  Her lover's tokens she would answer not—
'Twere well she should be strange with him
    somewhat :
A pretty babe, this Love,—but fie on it,
That would not suffer her lay it down a whit !
Appointed tryst defiantly she balked,
And with her lightest comrade lightly walked,
Who scared the chidden Love to hide apart,
And peep from some unnoticed corner of her
    heart.
She thought not of her lover, deem it not
(There yonder, in the hollow, that's *his* cot),
But she forgot not that he was forgot.
She saw him at his gate, yet stilled her tongue—
So weak she felt her, that she would feel strong,
And she must punish him for doing him wrong :
Passed, unoblivious of oblivion still ;
And, if she turned upon the brow o' the hill,
It was so openly, so lightly done,
You saw she thought he was not thought upon.
He through the gate went back in bitterness ;
She that night woke and stirred, with no distress,
Glad of her doing,—sedulous to be glad,
Lest perhaps her foolish heart suspect that it
    was sad.

PENELOPE

LOVE, like a wind, shook wide your blossomy eyes;
    You trembled, and your breath came sobbing-
        wise,
    For that you loved me.

You were so kind, so sweet, none could withhold
To adore, but that you were so strange, so cold,
    For that you loved me.

Like to a box of spikenard did you break
Your heart about my feet. What words you spake!
    For that you loved me.

Life fell to dust without me ; so you tried
All carefullest ways to drive me from your side,
    For that you loved me.

You gave yourself as children give, that weep
And snatch back, with—' I meant you not to keep ! '
    For that you loved me.

I am no woman, girl, nor ever knew
That love could teach all ways that hate could do
    To her that loved me.

Have less of love, or less of woman in
Your love, or loss may even from this begin—
    That you so love me.

PENELOPE

For, wild Penelope, the web you wove
You still unweave, unloving all your love.
    Is this to love me,

Or what rights have I that scorn could deny ?
Even of your love, alas, poor Love must die,
    If so you love me !

THE END OF IT

SHE did not love to love, but hated him
For making her to love ; and so her whim
From passion taught misprision to begin.
And all this sin
Was because love to cast out had no skill
Self, which was regent still.
Her own self-will made void her own self's will.

EPILOGUE

IF I have studied here in part
A tale as old as maiden's heart,
   'Tis that I do see herein
   Shadow of more piteous sin.

She, that but giving part, not whole,
Took even the part back, is the Soul:
   And that so disdainèd Lover—
   Best unthought, since Love is over.

To give the pledge, and yet be pined
That a pledge should have force to bind,
   This, O Soul, too often still
   Is the recreance of thy will!

Out of Love's arms to make fond chain,
And, because struggle bringeth pain,
   Hate Love for Love's sweet constraint,
   Is the way of Souls that faint.

Such a Soul, for saddest end,
Finds Love the foe in Love the friend;
   And—ah, grief incredible!—
   Treads the way of Heaven, to Hell.

ULTIMA

LOVE'S ALMSMAN PLAINETH
HIS FARE

YOU, Love's mendicancy who never tried,
　　How little of your almsman me you know !
　　Your little languid hand in mine you slide,
Like to a child says—' Kiss me and let me go ! '
And night for this is fretted with my tears,
　　While I :—' How soon this heavenly neck doth tire,
Bending to me from its transtellar spheres ! '
　　Ah, heart all kneaded out of honey and fire !
Who bound thee to a body nothing worth,
　　And shamed thee much with an unlovely soul,
That the most strainedest charity of earth
　　Distasteth soon to render back the whole
Of thine inflamèd sweets and gentilesse ?
　　Whereat, like an unpastured Titan, thou
Gnaw'st on thyself for famine's bitterness,
　　And leap'st against thy chain. Sweet Lady, how
Little a linking of the hand to you !
　　Though I should touch yours careless for a year,
Not one blue vein would lie divinelier blue
　　Upon your fragile temple, to unsphere
The seraphim for kisses ! Not one curve
　　Of your sad mouth would droop more sad and
　　　　sweet.
But little food Love's beggars needs must serve,
　　That eye your plenteous graces from the street.

LOVE'S ALMSMAN PLAINETH HIS FARE

A hand-clasp I must feed on for a night,
   A noon, although the untasted feast you lay,
To mock me, of your beauty. That you might
   Be lover for one space, and make essay
What 'tis to pass unsuppered to your couch,
   Keep fast from love all day ; and so be taught
The famine which these craving lines avouch !
   Ah ! miser of good things that cost thee naught,
How know'st thou poor men's hunger ?—Misery,
When I go doleless and unfed by thee !

A HOLOCAUST

*'No man ever attained supreme knowledge, unless his heart
had been torn up by the roots.'*

WHEN I presage the time shall come—yea, now
Perchance is come, when you shall fail from me,
Because the mighty spirit, to whom you vow
Faith of kin genius unrebukably,
Scourges my sloth ; and from your side dismissed
Henceforth this sad and most, most lonely soul
Must, marching fatally through pain and mist,
The God-bid levy of its powers enrol ;
When I presage that none shall hear the voice
From the great Mount that clangs my ordained
advance,
That sullen envy bade the churlish choice
Yourself shall say, and turn your altered glance ;—
O God ! Thou knowest if this heart of flesh
Quivers like broken entrails, when the wheel
Rolleth some dog in middle street, or fresh
Fruit when ye tear it bleeding from the peel ;
If my soul cries the uncomprehended cry
When the red agony oozed on Olivet.
Yet not for this, a caitiff, falter I,
Beloved whom I must lose, nor thence regret
The doubly-vouched and twin allegiance owed
To you in Heaven, and Heaven in you, Lady.
How could you hope, loose dealer with my God,
That I should keep for you my fealty ?
For still 'tis thus :—because I am so true,
My Fair, to Heaven, I am so true to you !

MY LADY THE TYRANNESS

ME since your fair ambition bows
Feodary to those gracious brows,
Is nothing mine will not confess
Your sovran sweet rapaciousness ?
Though use to the white yoke inures,
Half-petulant is
Your loving rebel for somewhat his,
Not yours, my love, not yours !

Behold my skies, which make with me
One passionate tranquillity !
Wrap thyself in them as a robe,
She shares them not ; their azures probe,
No countering wings thy flight endures.
Nay, they do stole
Me like an aura of her soul.
I yield them, love, for yours !

But mine these hills and fields, which put
Not on the sanctity of her foot.
Far off, my dear, far off the sweet
Grave *pianissimo* of your feet !
My earth, perchance, your sway abjures ?—
Your absence broods
O'er all, a subtler presence. Woods,
Fields, hills, all yours, all yours !

Nay then, I said, I have my thought,
Which never woman's reaching raught ;

MY LADY THE TYRANNESS

Being strong beyond a woman's might,
And high beyond a woman's height,
Shaped to my shape in all contours.—
I looked, and knew
No thought but you were garden to.
All yours, my love, all yours!

Meseemeth still, I have my life;
All-clement Her its resolute strife
Evades; contained, relinquishing
Her mitigating eyes; a thing
Which the whole girth of God secures.
Ah, fool, pause! pause!
I had no life, until it was
All yours, my love, all yours!

Yet, stern possession! I have my death,
Sole yielding up of my sole breath,
Which all within myself I die,
All in myself must cry the cry
Which the deaf body's wall immures.—
Thought fashioneth
My death without her.—Ah, even death
All yours, my love, all yours!

Death, then, be hers. I have my heaven,
For which no arm of hers has striven;
Which solitary I must choose,
And solitary win or lose.—
Ah, but not heaven my own endures!
I must perforce

ULTIMA

Taste you, my stream, in God your source,—
So steep my heaven in yours!

At last I said—I have my God,
Who doth desire me, though a clod,
And from His liberal Heaven shall He
Bar in mine arms His privacy.
Himself for mine Himself assures.—
None shall deny
God to be mine, but He and I
All yours, my love, all yours!

I have no fear at all lest I
Without her draw felicity.
God for His Heaven will not forego
Her whom I found such heaven below,
And she will train Him to her lures.
Naught, lady, I love
In you but more is loved above;
What made me, makes Him, yours.

' I, thy sought own, am I forgot ? '
Ha, thou ?—thou liest, I seek thee not.
Why what, thou painted parrot, Fame,
What have I taught thee but her name ?
Hear, thou slave Fame, while Time endures,
I give her thee ;
Page her triumphal name !—Lady,
Take her, the thrall is yours.

UNTO THIS LAST

A BOY'S young fancy taketh love
    Most simply, with the rind thereof ;
    A boy's young fancy tasteth more
The rind, than the deific core.
Ah, Sweet ! to cast away the slips
Of unessential rind, and lips
Fix on the immortal core, is well ;
But heard'st thou ever any tell
Of such a fool would take for food
Aspect and scent, however good,
Of sweetest core Love's orchards grow ?
Should such a phantast please him so,
Love where Love's reverent self denies
Love to feed, but with his eyes,
All the savour, all the touch,
Another's—was there ever such ?
Such were fool, if fool there be ;
Such fool was I, and was for thee !
But if the touch and savour too
Of this fruit—say, Sweet, of you—
You unto another give
For sacrosanct prerogative,
Yea, even scent and aspect were
Some elected Second's share ;
And one, gone mad, should rest content
With memory of show and scent ;
Would not thyself vow, if there sigh
Such a fool—say, Sweet, as I—
Treble frenzy it must be
Still to love, and to love thee ?

ULTIMA

Yet had I torn (man knoweth not,
Nor scarce the unweeping angels wot
Of such dread task the lightest part)
Her fingers from about my heart.
Heart, did we not think that she
Had surceased her tyranny ?
Heart, we bounded, and were free !
O sacrilegious freedom !—Till
She came, and taught my apostate will
The winnowed sweet mirth cannot guess
And tear-fined peace of hopelessness ;
Looked, spake, simply touched, and went.
Now old pain is fresh content,
Proved content is unproved pain.
Pangs fore-tempted, which in vain
I, faithless, have denied, now bud
To untempted fragrance and the mood
Of contrite heavenliness ; all days
Joy affrights me in my ways ;
Extremities of old delight
Afflict me with new exquisite
Virgin piercings of surprise,—
Stung by those wild brown bees, her eyes !

ULTIMUM

NOW in these last spent drops, slow, slower shed,
Love dies, Love dies, Love dies—ah, Love is
dead!
Sad Love in life, sore Love in agony,
Pale Love in death; while all his offspring songs,
Like children, versed not in death's chilly wrongs,
About him flit, frighted to see him lie
So still, who did not know that Love could die.
One lifts his wing, where dulls the vermeil all
Like clotting blood, and shrinks to find it cold,
And when she sees its lapse and nerveless fall
Clasps her fans, while her sobs ooze through the
webbèd gold.
Thereat all weep together, and their tears
Make lights like shivered moonlight on long waters.
Have peace, O piteous daughters!
He shall not wake more through the mortal years,
Nor comfort come to my soul widowèd,
Nor breath to your wild wings; for Love is dead!
I slew, that moan for him; he lifted me
Above myself, and that I might not be
Less than myself, need was that he should die;
Since Love that first did wing, now clogged me from
the sky.
Yet lofty Love being dead thus passeth base—
There is a soul of nobleness which stays,
The spectre of the rose: be comforted,
Songs, for the dust that dims his sacred head!
The days draw on too dark for Song or Love;
O peace, my songs, nor stir ye any wing!

ULTIMA

For lo, the thunder hushing all the grove,
And did Love live, not even Love could sing.

And, Lady, thus I dare to say,
Not all with you is passed away!
Beyond your star, still, still the stars are bright;
Beyond your highness, still I follow height;
Sole I go forth, yet still to my sad view,
Beyond your trueness, Lady, Truth stands true.
This wisdom sings my song with last firm breath,
Caught from the twisted lore of Love and Death,
The strange inwoven harmony that wakes
From Pallas' straying locks twined with her ægis-
    snakes :
' On him the unpetitioned heavens descend,
Who heaven on earth proposes not for end;
The perilous and celestial excess
Taking with peace, lacking with thankfulness.
Bliss in extreme befits thee not, until
Thou 'rt not extreme in bliss; be equal still :
Sweets to be granted think thyself unmeet
Till thou have learned to hold sweet not too sweet.'
This thing not far is he from wise in art
Who teacheth; nor who doth, from wise in heart.

AN ANTHEM OF EARTH

AN ANTHEM OF EARTH

PROEMION

IMMEASURABLE Earth!
Through the loud vast and populacy of Heaven,
Tempested with gold schools of ponderous orbs,
That cleav'st with deep-revolving harmonies
Passage perpetual, and behind thee draw'st
A furrow sweet, a cometary wake
Of trailing music! What large effluence,
Not sole the cloudy sighing of thy seas,
Nor thy blue-coifing air, encases thee
From prying of the stars, and the broad shafts
Of thrusting sunlight tempers? For, dropped near
From my removèd tour in the serene
Of utmost contemplation, I scent lives.
This is the efflux of thy rocks and fields,
And wind-cuffed forestage, and the souls of men,
And aura of all treaders over thee;
A sentient exhalation, wherein close
The odorous lives of many-throated flowers,
And each thing's mettle effused; that so thou wear'st,
Even like a breather on a frosty morn,
Thy proper suspiration. For I know,
Albeit, with custom-dulled perceivingness,
Nestled against thy breast, my sense not take
The breathings of thy nostrils, there 's no tree,
No grain of dust, nor no cold-seeming stone,
But wears a fume of its circumfluous self.
Thine own life and the lives of all that live,
The issue of thy loins,

AN ANTHEM OF EARTH

Is this thy gaberdine,
Wherein thou walkest through thy large demesne
And sphery pleasances,—
Amazing the unstalèd eyes of Heaven,
And us that still a precious seeing have
Behind this dim and mortal jelly.
                                            Ah !
If not in all too late and frozen a day
I come in rearward of the throats of song,
Unto the deaf sense of the agèd year
Singing with doom upon me ; yet give heed !
One poet with sick pinion, that still feels
Breath through the Orient gateways closing fast,
Fast closing t'ward the undelighted night !

ANTHEM

IN nescientness, in nescientness,
  Mother, we put these fleshly lendings on
  Thou yield'st to thy poor children ; took thy gift
Of life, which must, in all the after days,
Be craved again with tears,—
With fresh and still-petitionary tears.
Being once bound thine almsmen for that gift,
We are bound to beggary, nor our own can call
The journal dole of customary life,
But after suit obsequious for't to thee.
Indeed this flesh, O Mother,
A beggar's gown, a client's badging,
We find, which from thy hands we simply took,
Naught dreaming of the after penury,
In nescientness.

AN ANTHEM OF EARTH

In a little joy, in a little joy,
We wear awhile thy sore insignia,
Nor know thy heel o' the neck. O Mother ! Mother !
Then what use knew I of thy solemn robes,
But as a child to play with them ? I bade thee
Leave thy great husbandries, thy grave designs,
Thy tedious state which irked my ignorant years,
Thy winter-watches, suckling of the grain,
Severe premeditation taciturn
Upon the brooded Summer, thy chill cares,
And all thy ministries majestical,
To sport with me, thy darling. Thought I not
Thou sett'st thy seasons forth processional
To pamper me with pageant,—thou thyself
My fellow-gamester, appanage of mine arms ?
Then what wild Dionysia I, young Bacchanal,
Danced in thy lap ! Ah for thy gravity !
Then, O Earth, thou rang'st beneath me,
Rocked to Eastward, rocked to Westward,
Even with the shifted
Poise and footing of my thought !
I brake through thy doors of sunset,
Ran before the hooves of sunrise,
Shook thy matron tresses down in fancies
Wild and wilful
As a poet's hand could twine them ;
Caught in my fantasy's crystal chalice
The Bow, as its cataract of colours
Plashed to thee downward ;
Then when thy circuit swung to nightward,
Night the abhorrèd, night was a new dawning,

AN ANTHEM OF EARTH

Celestial dawning
Over the ultimate marges of the soul;
Dusk grew turbulent with fire before me,
And like a windy arras waved with dreams.
Sleep I took not for my bedfellow,
Who could waken
To a revel, an inexhaustible
Wassail of orgiac imageries;
Then while I wore thy sore insignia
In a little joy, O Earth, in a little joy;
Loving thy beauty in all creatures born of thee,
Children, and the sweet-essenced body of woman
Feeling not yet upon my neck thy foot,
But breathing warm of thee as infants breathe
New from their mother's morning bosom. So I,
Risen from thee, restless winnower of the heaven,
Most Hermes-like, did keep
My vital and resilient path, and felt
The play of wings about my fledgèd heel—
Sure on the verges of precipitous dream,
Swift in its springing
From jut to jut of inaccessible fancies,
In a little joy.

In a little thought, in a little thought,
We stand and eye thee in a grave dismay,
With sad and doubtful questioning, when first
Thou speak'st to us as men : like sons who hear
Newly their mother's history, unthought
Before, and say—' She is not as we dreamed :
Ah me ! we are beguiled ! ' What art thou, then,

AN ANTHEM OF EARTH

That art not our conceiving ? Art thou not
Too old for thy young children ? Or perchance,
Keep'st thou a youth perpetual-burnishable
Beyond thy sons decrepit ? It is long
Since Time was first a fledgeling ;
Yet thou may'st be but as a pendant bulla
Against his stripling bosom swung. Alack !
For that we seem indeed
To have slipped the world's great leaping-time,
        and come
Upon thy pinched and dozing days : these weeds,
These corporal leavings, thou not cast'st us new,
Fresh from thy craftship, like the lilies' coats,
But foist'st us off
With hasty tarnished piecings negligent,
Snippets and waste
From old ancestral wearings,
That have seen sorrier usage ; remainder-flesh
After our father's surfeits ; nay with chinks,
Some of us, that, if speech may have free leave,
Our souls go out at elbows. We are sad
With more than our sires' heaviness, and with
More than their weakness weak ; we shall not be
Mighty with all their mightiness, nor shall not
Rejoice with all their joy. Ay, Mother ! Mother !
What is this Man, thy darling kissed and cuffed,
Thou lustingly engender'st,
To sweat, and make his brag, and rot,
Crowned with all honour and all shamefulness ?
From nightly towers
He dogs the secret footsteps of the heavens,

Sifts in his hands the stars, weighs them as gold-dust,
And yet is he successive unto nothing
But patrimony of a little mold,
And entail of four planks. Thou hast made his mouth
Avid of all dominion and all mightiness,
All sorrow, all delight, all topless grandeurs,
All beauty, and all starry majesties,
And dim transtellar things ;—even that it may,
Filled in the ending with a puff of dust,
Confess—' It is enough.' The world left empty
What that poor mouthful crams. His heart is builded
For pride, for potency, infinity,
All heights, all deeps, and all immensities,
Arrased with purple like the house of kings,—
To stall the grey-rat, and the carrion-worm
Statelily lodge. Mother of mysteries !
Sayer of dark sayings in a thousand tongues,
Who bringest forth no saying yet so dark
As we ourselves, thy darkest ! We the young,
In a little thought, in a little thought,
At last confront thee, and ourselves in thee,
And wake disgarmented of glory : as one
On a mount standing, and against him stands,
On the mount adverse, crowned with westering rays,
The golden sun, and they two brotherly
Gaze each on each ;
He faring down
To the dull vale, his Godhead peels from him
Till he can scarcely spurn the pebble—
For nothingness of new-found mortality—
That mutinies against his gallèd foot.

AN ANTHEM OF EARTH

Littly he sets him to the daily way,
With all around the valleys growing grave,
And known things changed and strange ; but he
    holds on,
Though all the land of light be widowèd,
In a little thought.

In a little strength, in a little strength,
We affront thy unveiled face intolerable,
Which yet we do sustain.
Though I the Orient never more shall feel
Break like a clash of cymbals, and my heart
Clang through my shaken body like a gong ;
Nor ever more with spurted feet shall tread
I' the winepresses of song ; naught 's truly lost
That moulds to sprout forth gain : now I have on me
The high Phœbean priesthood, and that craves
An unrash utterance ; not with flaunted hem
May the Muse enter in behind the veil,
Nor, though we hold the sacred dances good,
Shall the holy Virgins mænadize : ruled lips
Befit a votaress Muse.
Thence with no mutable, nor no gelid love,
I keep, O Earth, thy worship,
Though life slow, and the sobering Genius change
To a lamp his gusty torch. What though no more
Athwart its roseal glow
Thy face look forth triumphal ? Thou putt'st on
Strange sanctities of pathos ; like this knoll
Made derelict of day,
Couchant and shadowèd

AN ANTHEM OF EARTH

Under dim Vesper's overloosened hair :
This, where embossèd with the half-blown seed
The solemn purple thistle stands in grass
Grey as an exhalation, when the bank
Holds mist for water in the nights of Fall.
Not to the boy, although his eyes be pure
As the prime snowdrop is
Ere the rash Phœbus break her cloister
Of sanctimonious snow ;
Or Winter fasting sole on Himalay
Since those dove-nuncioed days
When Asia rose from bathing ;
Not to such eyes,
Uneuphrasied with tears, the hierarchical
Vision lies unoccult, rank under rank
Through all create down-wheeling, from the Throne
Even to the bases of the pregnant ooze.
This is the enchantment, this the exaltation,
The all-compensating wonder,
Giving to common things wild kindred
With the gold-tesserate floors of Jove ;
Linking such heights and such humilities
Hand in hand in ordinal dances,
That I do think my tread,
Stirring the blossoms in the meadow-grass,
Flickers the unwithering stars.
This to the shunless fardel of the world
Nerves my uncurbèd back : that I endure,
The monstrous Temple's moveless caryatid,
With wide eyes calm upon the whole of things,
In a little strength.

AN ANTHEM OF EARTH

In a little sight, in a little sight,
We learn from what in thee is credible
The incredible, with bloody clutch and feet
Clinging the painful juts of jaggèd faith.
Science, old noser in its prideful straw,
That with anatomising scalpel tents
Its three-inch of thy skin, and brags ' All 's bare '—
The eyeless worm, that, boring, works the soil,
Making it capable for the crops of God ;
Against its own dull will
Ministers poppies to our troublous thought,
A Balaam come to prophecy,—parables,
Nor of its parable itself is ware,
Grossly unwotting ; all things has expounded,
Reflux and influx, counts the sepulchre
The seminary of being, and extinction
The Ceres of existence : it discovers
Life in putridity, vigour in decay ;
Dissolution even, and disintegration,
Which in our dull thoughts symbolize disorder,
Finds in God's thoughts irrefragable order,
And admirable the manner of our corruption
As of our health. It grafts upon the cypress
The tree of Life—Death dies on his own dart
Promising to our ashes perpetuity,
And to our perishable elements
Their proper imperishability ; extracting
Medicaments from out mortality
Against too mortal cogitation ; till
Even of the *caput mortuum* we do thus
Make a *memento vivere*. To such uses

AN ANTHEM OF EARTH

I put the blinding knowledge of the fool,
Who in no order seeth ordinance ;
Nor thrust my arm in nature shoulder-high,
And cry—' There's naught beyond ! ' How should
    I so,
That cannot with these arms of mine engirdle
All which I am ; that am a foreigner
In mine own region ? Who the chart shall draw
Of the strange courts and vaulty labyrinths,
The spacious tenements and wide pleasances,
Innumerable corridors far-withdrawn,
Wherein I wander darkling, of myself ?
Darkling I wander, nor I dare explore
The long arcane of those dim catacombs,
Where the rat memory does its burrows make,
Close-seal them as I may, and my stolen tread
Starts populace, a *gens lucifuga ;*
That too strait seems my mind my mind to hold,
And I myself incontinent of me.
Then go I, my foul-venting ignorance
With scabby sapience plastered, aye forsooth !
Clap my wise foot-rule to the walls o' the world,
And vow—*A goodly house, but something ancient,*
And I can find no Master ?   Rather, nay,
By baffled seeing, something I divine
Which baffles, and a seeing set beyond ;
And so with strenuous gazes sounding down,
Like to the day-long porer on a stream,
Whose last look is his deepest, I beside
This slow perpetual Time stand patiently,
In a little sight.

AN ANTHEM OF EARTH

In a little dust, in a little dust,
Earth, thou reclaim'st us, who do all our lives
Find of thee but Egyptian villeinage.
Thou dost this body, this enhavocked realm,
Subject to ancient and ancestral shadows ;
Descended passions sway it ; it is distraught
With ghostly usurpation, dinned and fretted
With the still-tyrannous dead ; a haunted tenement,
Peopled from barrows and outworn ossuaries.
Thou giv'st us life not half so willingly
As thou undost thy giving ; thou that teem'st
The stealthy terror of the sinuous pard,
The lion maned with curlèd puissance,
The serpent, and all fair strong beasts of ravin,
Thyself most fair and potent beast of ravin,
And thy great eaters thou, the greatest, eat'st.
Thou hast devoured mammoth and mastodon,
And many a floating bank of fangs,
The scaly scourges of thy primal brine,
And the tower-crested plesiosaure.
Thou fill'st thy mouth with nations, gorgest slow
On purple æons of kings ; man's hulking towers
Are carcase for thee, and to modern sun
Disglutt'st their splintered bones.
Rabble of Pharaohs and Arsacidæ
Keep their cold house within thee ; thou hast sucked
    down
How many Ninevehs and Hecatompyloi,
And perished cities whose great phantasmata
O'erbrow the silent citizens of Dis :—
Hast not thy fill ?

AN ANTHEM OF EARTH

Tarry awhile, lean Earth, for thou shalt drink,
Even till thy dull throat sicken,
The draught thou grow'st most fat on ; hear'st thou
    not
The world's knives bickering in their sheaths ? O
    patience !
Much offal of a foul world comes thy way,
And man's superfluous cloud shall soon be laid
In a little blood.

In a little peace, in a little peace,
Thou dost rebate thy rigid purposes
Of imposed being, and relenting, mend'st
Too much, with naught. The westering Phœbus'
    horse
Paws i' the lucent dust as when he shocked
The East with rising ; O how may I trace
In this decline that morning when we did
Sport 'twixt the claws of newly-whelped existence,
Which had not yet learned rending ? we did then
Divinely stand, not knowing yet against us
Sentence had passed of life, nor commutation
Petitioning into death. What 's he that of
The Free State argues ? Tellus, bid him stoop,
Even where the low *hic jacet* answers him ;
Thus low, O Man ! there 's freedom's seignory,
Tellus' most reverend sole free commonweal,
And model deeply-policied : there none
Stands on precedence, nor ambitiously
Woos the impartial worm, whose favours kiss
With liberal largesse all ; there each is free

To be e'en what he must, which here did strive
So much to be he could not ; there all do
Their uses just, with no flown questioning.
To be took by the hand of equal earth
They doff her livery, slip to the worm,
Which lacqueys them, their suits of maintenance,
And, that soiled workaday apparel cast,
Put on condition : Death's ungentle buffet
Alone makes ceremonial manumission ;
So are the heavenly statutes set, and those
Uranian tables of the primal Law.
In a little peace, in a little peace,
Like fierce beasts that a common thirst makes
    brothers,
We draw together to one hid dark lake ;
In a little peace, in a little peace,
We drain with all our burthens of dishonour
Into the cleansing sands o' the thirsty grave.
The fiery pomps, brave exhalations,
And all the glistering shows o' the seeming world,
Which the sight aches at, we unwinking see
Through the smoked glass of Death ; Death, where-
    with 's fined
The muddy wine of life ; that earth doth purge
Of her plethora of man ; Death, that doth flush
The cumbered gutters of humanity ;
Nothing, of nothing king, with front uncrowned,
Whose hand holds crownets ; playmate swart o' the
    strong ;
Tenebrous moon that flux and refluence draws
Of the high-tided man ; skull-housèd asp

AN ANTHEM OF EARTH

That stings the heel of kings ; true Fount of Youth,
Where he that dips is deathless ; being's drone-pipe ;
Whose nostril turns to blight the shrivelled stars,
And thicks the lusty breathing of the sun ;
Pontifical Death, that doth the crevasse bridge
To the steep and trifid God ; one mortal birth
That broker is of immortality.
Under this dreadful brother uterine,
This kinsman feared, Tellus, behold me come,
Thy son stern-nursed ; who mortal-motherlike,
To turn thy weanlings' mouth averse, embitter'st
Thine over-childed breast. Now, mortal-sonlike,
I thou hast suckled, Mother, I at last
Shall sustenant be to thee. Here I untrammel,
Here I pluck loose the body's cerementing,
And break the tomb of life ; here I shake off
The bur o' the world, man's congregation shun,
And to the antique order of the dead
I take the tongueless vows : my cell is set
Here in thy bosom ; my little trouble is ended
In a little peace.

MISCELLANEOUS ODES

LAUS AMARA DOLORIS

IMPLACABLE sweet dæmon, Poetry,
What have I lost for thee !
Whose lips too sensitively well
Have shaped thy shrivelling oracle.
So much as I have lost, O world, thou hast,
And for thy plenty I am waste ;
Ah, count, O world, my cost,
Ah, count, O world, thy gain,
For thou hast nothing gained but I have lost !
And ah, my loss is such,
If thou have gained as much
Thou hast even harvest of Egyptian years,
And that great overflow which gives thee grain—
The bitter Nilus of my risen tears !

I witness call the austere goddess, Pain,
Whose mirrored image trembles where it lies
In my confronting eyes,
If I have learned her sad and solemn scroll :—
Have I neglected her high sacrifice,
Spared my heart's children to the sacred knife,
Or turned her customed footing from my soul ?
Yea, thou pale Ashtaroth who rul'st my life,
Of all my offspring thou hast had the whole.
One after one they passed at thy desire
To sacrificial sword, or sacrificial fire ;
All, all,—save one, the sole.
One have I hid apart,
The latest-born and sweetest of my heart,
From thy requiring eyes.

O hope, most futile of futilities !
Thine iron summons comes again,
O inevadible Pain !
Not faithless to my pact, I yield :—'tis here,
That solitary and fair,
That most sweet, last, and dear ;
Swerv'st thou ? behold, I swerve not :—strike, nor
    spare !
Not my will shudders, but my flesh,
In awful secrecy to hear
The wind of thy great treading sweep afresh
Athwart my face, and agitate my hair.
The ultimate unnerving dearness take,
The extreme rite of abnegation make,
And sum in one all renderings that were.

The agony is done,
Her footstep passes on ;—
The unchilded chambers of my heart rest bare.
The love, but not the loved, remains ;
As where a flower has pressed a leaf
The page yet keeps the trace and stains.
For thy delight, world, one more grief,
My world, one loss more for thy gains !

Yet, yet, ye few, to whom is given
This weak singing, I have learned
Ill the starry roll of heaven,
Were this all that I discerned
Or of Poetry or of Pain.
Song ! turn on thy hinge again !

LAUS AMARA DOLORIS

Thine alternate panel showed,
Give the Ode a Palinode !
Pain, not thou an Ashtaroth,
Glutted with a bloody rite,
But the icy bath that doth
String the slack sinews loosened with delight.
O great Key-bearer and Keeper
Of the treasuries of God !
Wisdom's gifts are buried deeper
Than the arm of man can go,
Save thou show
First the way, and turn the sod.
The poet's crown, with misty weakness tarnished,
In thy golden fire is burnished
To round with more illustrious gleam his forehead.
And when with sacrifice of costliest cost
On my heart's altar is the Eterne adorèd,
The fire from heaven consumes the holocaust.
Nay, to vicegerence o'er the wide-confined
And mutinous principate of man's restless mind
With thine anointing oils the singer is designed :
To that most desolate station
Thine is his deep and dolorous consecration.
Oh, where thy chrism shall dry upon my brow,
By that authentic sign I know
The sway is parted from this tenuous hand :
And all the wonted dreams that rankèd stand,
The high majestic state,
And cloud-consorting towers of visionary land,
To some young usurpation needs must go ;
And I am all unsceptred of command.

Disdiademed I wait
To speak with sieging Death, mine enemy, in tne gate.

Preceptress in the wars of God !
His tyros draw the unmortal sword,
And their celestial virtue exercise,
Beneath thy rigorous eyes.
Thou severe bride, with the glad suit adored
Of many a lover whose love is unto blood ;
Every jewel in their crown
Thy lapidary hand does own ;
Nor that warm jacinth of the heart can put
Its lustres forth, till it be cut.
Thou settest thine abode
A portress in the gateways of all love,
And tak'st the toll of joys ; no maid is wed,
But thou dost draw the curtains of her bed.
Yea, on the brow of mother and of wife
Descends thy confirmation from above,
A Pentecostal flame ; love's holy bread,
Consecrated,
Not sacramental is, but through thy leaven.

Thou pacest either frontier where our life
Marches with God's ; both birth and death are given
Into thy lordship ; those debated lands
Are subject to thy hands :
The border-warden, thou, of Heaven—
Yea, that same awful angel with the glaive
Which in disparadising orbit swept
Lintel and pilaster and architrave

LAUS AMARA DOLORIS

Of Eden-gates, and forth before it drave
The primal pair, then first whose startled eyes,
With pristine drops o' the no less startled skies
Their own commingling, wept ;—
With strange affright
Sin knew the bitter first baptismal rite.

Save through thy ministry man is not fed ;
Thou uninvoked presid'st, and unconfest,
The mistress of his feast :
From the earth we gain our bread, and—like the bread
Dropt and regatherèd
By a child crost and thwart,
Whom need makes eat, though sorely weep he for't—
It tastes of dust and tears.

Iron Ceres of an earth where, since the Curse,
Man has had power perverse
Beside God's good to set his evil seed !
Those shining acres of the musket-spears—
Where flame and wither with swift intercease
Flowers of red sleep that not the corn-field bears—
Do yield thee minatory harvest, when
Unto the fallow time of sensual ease
Implacably succeed
The bristling issues of the sensual deed ;
And like to meteors from a rotting fen
The fiery pennons flit o'er the stagnation
Of the world's sluggish and putrescent life,
Misleading to engulfing desolation
And blind, retributive, unguessing strife,
The fatal footsteps of pursuing men.

Thy pall in purple sovereignty was dipt
Beneath the tree of Golgotha ;
And from the Hand, wherein the reed was clipt,
Thy bare and antique sceptre thou dost draw.
That God-sprung Lover to thy front allows,
Fairest, the bloody honour of His brows,
The great reversion of that diadem
Which did His drenched locks hem.
For the predestinated Man of Grief,
O regnant Pain, to thee
His subject sway elected to enfeoff ;
And from thy sad conferring to endure
The sanguine state of His investiture ;
Yea, at thy hand, most sombre suzerain,
That dreadful crown He held in fealty ;
O Queen of Calvary,
Holy and terrible, anointed Pain !

A CAPTAIN OF SONG

(ON A PORTRAIT OF COVENTRY PATMORE
BY J. S. SARGENT, R.A.)

LOOK on him. This is he whose works ye know ;
    Ye have adored, thanked, loved him,—no, not
    him !
But that of him which proud portentous woe
To its own grim
Presentment was not potent to subdue,
Nor all the reek of Erebus to dim.
This, and not him, ye knew.
Look on him now. Love, worship if ye can,
The very man.
Ye may not. He has trod the ways afar,
The fatal ways of parting and farewell,
Where all the paths of painèd greatness are ;
Where round and always round
The abhorrèd words resound,
The words accursed of comfortable men,—
' For ever ' ; and infinite glooms intolerable
With spacious replication give again,
And hollow jar,
The words abhorred of comfortable men.
You the stern pities of the gods debar
To drink where he has drunk—
The moonless mere of sighs,
And pace the places infamous to tell,
Where God wipes not the tears from any eyes,
Where-through the ways of dreadful greatness are.

He knows the perilous rout
That all those ways about
Sink into doom, and sinking, still are sunk.
And if his sole and solemn term thereout
He has attained, to love ye shall not dare
One who has journeyed there ;
Ye shall mark well
The mighty cruelties which arm and mar
That countenance of control,
With minatory warnings of a soul
That hath to its own selfhood been most fell,
And is not weak to spare :
And lo, that hair
Is blanchèd with the travel-heats of hell.

If any be
That shall with rites of reverent piety
Approach this strong
Sad soul of sovereign Song,
Nor fail and falter with the intimidate throng ;
If such there be,
These, these are only they
Have trod the self-same way ;
The never-twice revolving portals heard
Behind them clang infernal, and that word
Abhorrèd sighed of kind mortality,
As he—
Ah, even as he !

AGAINST URANIA

LO, I, Song's most true lover, plain me sore
 That worse than other women she can deceive,
 For she being goddess, I have given her more
Than mortal ladies from their loves receive ;
And first of her embrace
She was not coy, and gracious were her ways,
That I forgot all virgins to adore ;
Nor did I greatly grieve
To bear through arid days
The pretty foil of her divine delays ;
And one by one to cast
Life, love, and health,
Content, and wealth,
Before her, thinking ever on her praise.
Until at last
Naught had I left she would be gracious for.
Now of her cozening I complain me sore,
Seeing her uses,
That still, more constantly she is pursued,
And straitlier wooed,
Her only-adorèd favour more refuses,
And leaves me to implore
Remembered boon in bitterness of blood.

From mortal woman thou may'st know full well,
O poet, that dost deem the fair and tall
Urania of her ways not mutable,
What things shall thee befall
When thou art toilèd in her sweet, wild spell.

Do they strow for thy feet
A little tender favour and deceit
Over the sudden mouth of hidden hell ?—
As more intolerable
Her pit, as her first kiss is heavenlier-sweet.
Are they, the more thou sigh,
Still the more watchful-cruel to deny ?—
Know this, that in her service thou shalt learn
How harder than the heart of woman is
The immortal cruelty
Of the high goddesses.
True is his witness who doth witness this,
Whose gaze too early fell—
Nor thence shall turn,
Nor in those fires shall cease to weep and burn—
Upon her ruinous eyes and ineludible.

TO THE ENGLISH MARTYRS

RAIN, rain on Tyburn tree,
    Red rain a-falling ;
    Dew, dew on Tyburn tree,
Red dew on Tyburn tree,
And the swart bird a-calling.
The shadow lies on England now
Of the deathly-fruited bough :
Cold and black with malison
Lies between the land and sun ;
Putting out the sun, the bough
Shades England now !

The troubled heavens do wan with care,
And burthened with the earth's despair
Shiver a-cold ; the starvèd heaven
Has want, with wanting man bereaven.
Blest fruit of the unblest bough,
Aid the land that smote you, now !
That feels the sentence and the curse
Ye died if so ye might reverse.
When God was stolen from out man's mouth,
Stolen was the bread ; then hunger and drouth
Went to and fro ; began the wail,
Struck root the poor-house and the jail.
Ere cut the dykes, let through that flood,
Ye writ the protest with your blood ;
Against this night—wherein our breath
Withers, and the toiled heart perisheth,—
Entered the *caveat* of your death.

Christ, in the form of His true Bride,
Again hung pierced and crucified,
And groaned, ' I thirst ! ' Not still ye stood,—
Ye had your hearts, ye had your blood ;
And pouring out the eager cup,—
' The wine is weak, yet, Lord Christ, sup ! '
Ah, blest ! who bathed the parchèd Vine
With richer than His Cana-wine,
And heard, your most sharp supper past :
' Ye kept the best wine to the last ! '

Ah, happy who
That sequestered secret knew,
How sweeter than bee-haunted dells
The blosmy blood of martyrs smells !
Who did upon the scaffold's bed,
The ceremonial steel between you, wed
With God's grave proxy, high and reverend Death ;
Or felt about your neck, sweetly,
(While the dull horde
Saw but the unrelenting cord)
The Bridegroom's arm, and that long kiss
That kissed away your breath, and claimed you His.
You did, with thrift of holy gain,
Unvenoming the sting of pain,
Hive its sharp heather-honey. Ye
Had sentience of the mystery
To make Abaddon's hookèd wings
Buoy you up to starry things ;
Pain of heart, and pain of sense,
Pain the scourge, ye taught to cleanse ;

TO THE ENGLISH MARTYRS

Pain the loss became possessing ;
Pain the curse was pain the blessing.
Chains, rack, hunger, solitude—these,
Which did your soul from earth release,
Left it free to rush upon
And merge in its compulsive Sun.
Desolated, bruised, forsaken,
Nothing taking, all things taken,
Lacerated and tormented,
The stifled soul, in naught contented,
On all hands straitened, cribbed, denied,
Can but fetch breath o' the Godward side.
Oh to me, give but to me
That flower of felicity,
Which on your topmost spirit ware
The difficult and snowy air
Of high refusal ! and the heat
Of central love which fed with sweet
And holy fire i' the frozen sod
Roots that had ta'en hold on God.

Unwithering youth in you renewed
Those rosy waters of your blood,—
The true *Fons Juventutis ;* ye
Pass with conquest that Red Sea,
And stretch out your victorious hand
Over the Fair and Holy Land.
O, by the Church's pondering art
Late set and named upon the chart
Of her divine astronomy,
Though your influence from on high

Long ye shed unnoted ! Bright
New cluster in our Northern night,
Cleanse from its pain and undelight
An impotent and tarnished hymn,
Whose marish exhalations dim
Splendours they would transfuse ! And thou
Kindle the words which blot thee now,
Over whose sacred corse unhearsed
Europe veiled her face, and cursed
The regal mantle grained in gore
Of genius, freedom, faith, and More !

Ah, happy Fool of Christ, unawed
By familiar sanctities,
You served your Lord at holy ease !
Dear Jester in the Courts of God—
In whose spirit, enchanting yet,
Wisdom and love, together met,
Laughed on each other for content !
That an inward merriment,
An inviolate soul of pleasure,
To your motions taught a measure
All your days ; which tyrant king,
Nor bonds, nor any bitter thing
Could embitter or perturb ;
No daughter's tears, nor, more acerb,
A daughter's frail declension from
Thy serene example, come
Between thee and thy much content.
Nor could the last sharp argument
Turn thee from thy sweetest folly ;

TO THE ENGLISH MARTYRS

To the keen *accolade* and holy
Thou didst bend low a sprightly knee,
And jest Death out of gravity
As a too sad-visaged friend ;
So, jocund, passing to the end
Of thy laughing martyrdom ;
And now from travel art gone home
Where, since gain of thee was given,
Surely there is more mirth in heaven !

Thus, in Fisher and in thee,
Arose the purple dynasty,
The anointed Kings of Tyburn tree ;
High in act and word each one :
He that spake—and to the sun
Pointed—' I shall shortly be
Above yon fellow.' He too, he
No less high of speech and brave,
Whose word was : ' Though I shall have
Sharp dinner, yet I trust in Christ
To have a most sweet supper.' Priced
Much by men that utterance was
Of the doomed Leonidas,—
Not more exalt than these, which note
Men who thought as Shakespeare wrote.

But more lofty eloquence
Than is writ by poets' pens
Lives in your great deaths : O these
Have more fire than poesies !
And more ardent than all ode,
The pomps and raptures of your blood !

By that blood ye hold in fee
This earth of England ; Kings are ye :
And ye have armies—Want, and Cold,
And heavy Judgements manifold
Hung in the unhappy air, and Sins
That the sick gorge to heave begins,
Agonies, and Martyrdoms,
Love, Hope, Desire, and all that comes
From the unwatered soul of man
Gaping on God. These are the van
Of conquest, these obey you ; these,
And all the strengths of weaknesses,
That brazen walls disbed. Your hand,
Princes, put forth to the command,
And levy upon the guilty land
Your saving wars ; on it go down,
Black beneath God's and heaven's frown ;
Your prevalent approaches make
With unsustainable Grace, and take
Captive the land that captived you ;
To Christ enslave ye and subdue
Her so bragged freedom : for the crime
She wrought on you in antique time,
Parcel the land among you : reign,
Viceroys to your sweet Suzerain !
Till she shall know
This lesson in her overthrow :
Hardest servitude has he
That 's jailed in arrogant liberty ;
And freedom, spacious and unflawed,
Who is walled about with God.

ODE *for the* DIAMOND JUBILEE
OF QUEEN VICTORIA, 1897

NIGHT; and the street a corpse beneath the
    moon,
      Upon the threshold of the jubilant day
That was to follow soon ;
Thickened with inundating dark
'Gainst which the drowning lamps kept struggle ;
    pole
And plank cast rigid shadows ; 'twas a stark
Thing waiting for its soul,
The bones of the preluded pomp. I saw
In the cloud-sullied moon a pale array,
A lengthened apparition, slowly draw ;
And as it came,
Brake all the street in phantom flame
Of flag and flower and hanging, shadowy show
Of the to-morrow's glories, as might suit
A pageant of the dead ; and spectral bruit
I heard, where stood the dead to watch the dead,
The long Victorian line that passed with printless
    tread.

First went the holy poets, two on two,
And music, sown along the hardened ground,
Budded like frequence of glad daisies, where
Those sacred feet did fare ;
Arcadian pipe, and psaltery, around,

And stringèd viol, sound
To make for them melodious due.
In the first twain of those great ranks of death
Went One, the impress recent on his hair
Where it was dinted by the Laureate wreath :
Who sang those goddesses with splendours bare
On Ida hill, before the Trojan boy ;
And many a lovely lay,
Where Beauty did her beauties unarray
In conscious song. I saw young Love his plumes deploy,
And shake their shivering lustres, till the night
Was sprinkled and bedropt with starry play
Of versicoloured light,
To see that Poet pass who sang him well ;
And I could hear his heart
Throb like the after-vibrance of a bell.

A Strength beside this Beauty, Browning went,
With shrewd looks and intent,
And meditating still some gnarlèd theme.
Then came, somewhat apart,
In a fastidious dream,
Arnold, with a half-discontented calm,
Binding up wounds, but pouring in no balm.
The fervid breathing of Elizabeth
Broke on Christina's gentle-taken breath.
Rossetti, whose heart stirred within his breast
Like lightning in a cloud, a Spirit without rest,
Came on disranked ; Song's hand was in his hair,
Lest Art should have withdrawn him from the band,
Save for her strong command ;

And in his eyes high Sadness made its lair.
Last came a Shadow tall, with drooping lid,
Which yet not hid
The steel-like flashing of his armèd glance ;
Alone he did advance,
And all the throngs gave room
For one that looked with such a captain's mien.
A scornful smile lay keen
On lips that, living, prophesied of doom ;
His one hand held a lightning-bolt, the other
A cup of milk and honey blent with fire ;
It seemed as in that quire
He had not, nor desired not, any brother.
A space his alien eye surveyed the pride
Of meditated pomp, as one that much
Disdained the sight, methought ; then, at a touch,
He turned the heel, and sought with shadowy stride
His station in the dim,
Where the sole-thoughted Dante waited him.

What throngs illustrious next, of Art and Prose,
Too long to tell ! But other music rose
When came the sabre's children : they who led
The iron-throated harmonies of war,
The march resounding of the armèd line,
And measured movement of battalia :
Accompanied their tread
No harps, no pipes of soft Arcadia,
But—borne to me afar—
The tramp of squadrons, and the bursting mine,

The shock of steel, the volleying rifle-crack,
And echoes out of ancient battles dead.
So Cawnpore unto Alma thundered back,
And Delhi's cannon roared to Gujerat :
Carnage through all those iron vents gave out
Her thousand-mouthèd shout.
As balefire answering balefire is unfurled,
From mountain-peaks, to tell the foe's approaches,
So ran that battle-clangour round the world,
From famous field to field
So that reverberated war was tossed ;
And—in the distance lost—
Across the plains of France and hills of Spain
It swelled once more to birth,
And broke on me again,
The voice of England's glories girdling in the earth.

It caught like fire the main,
Where rending planks were heard, and broadsides
        pealed,
That shook were all the seas,
Which feared, and thought on Nelson. For with
        them
That struck the Russ, that brake the Mutineer,
And smote the stiff Sikh to his knee,—with these
Came they that kept our England's sea-swept hem,
And held afar from her the foreign fear.
After them came
They who pushed back the ocean of the Unknown,
And fenced some strand of knowledge for our own
Against the outgoing sea

THE VICTORIAN ODE

Of ebbing mystery ;
And on their banner ' Science ' blazoned shone.
The rear were they that wore the statesman's fame,
From Melbourne, to
The arcane face of the much-wrinkled Jew.

Lo, in this day we keep the yesterdays,
And those great dead of the Victorian line.
They passed, they passed, but cannot pass away,
For England feels them in her blood like wine.
She was their mother, and she is their daughter,
This Lady of the water,
And from their loins she draws the greatness which
    they were.
And still their wisdom sways,
Their power lives in her.
Their thews it is, England, that lift thy sword,
They are the splendour, England, in thy song,
They sit unbidden at thy council-board,
Their fame doth compass all thy coasts from wrong,
And in thy sinews they are strong.
Their absence is a presence and a guest
In this day's feast ;
This living feast is also of the dead,
And this, O England, is thine All Souls' Day.
And when thy cities flake the night with flames,
Thy proudest torches yet shall be their names.

O royal England ! happy child
Of such a more than regal line ;
Be it said

Fair right of jubilee is thine ;
And surely thou art unbeguiled
If thou keep with mirth and play,
With dance, and jollity, and praise,
Such a To-day which sums such Yesterdays.
Pour to the joyless ones thy joy, thy oil
And wine to such as faint and toil.
And let thy vales make haste to be more green
Than any vales are seen
In less auspicious lands,
And let thy trees clap all their leafy hands,
And let thy flowers be gladder far of hue
Than flowers of other regions may ;
Let the rose, with her fragrance sweetened through,
Flush as young maidens do,
With their own inward blissfulness at play.
And let the sky twinkle an eagerer blue
Over our English isle
Than any otherwhere ;
Till strangers shall behold, and own that she is fair.
Play up, play up, ye birds of minstrel June,
Play up your reel, play up your giddiest spring,
And trouble every tree with lusty tune,
Whereto our hearts shall dance
For overmuch pleasance,
And children's running make the earth to sing.
And ye soft winds, and ye white-fingered beams,
Aid ye her to invest,
Our queenly England, in all circumstance
Of fair and feat adorning to be drest ;
Kirtled in jocund green,

THE VICTORIAN ODE

Which does befit a Queen,
And like our spirits cast forth lively gleams :
And let her robe be goodly garlanded
With store of florets white and florets red,
With store of florets white and florets gold,
A fair thing to behold ;
Intrailed with the white blossom and the blue,
A seemly thing to view !
And thereunto,
Set over all a woof of lawny air,
From her head wavering to her sea-shod feet,
Which shall her lovely beauty well complete,
And grace her much to wear.

Lo, she is dressed, and lo, she cometh forth,
Our stately Lady of the North ;
Lo, how she doth advance,
In her most sovereign eye regard of puissance,
And tiar'd with conquest her prevailing brow,
While nations to her bow.
Come hither, proud and ancient East,
Gather ye to this Lady of the North,
And sit down with her at her solemn feast,
Upon this culminant day of all her days ;
For ye have heard the thunder of her goings-forth,
And wonder of her large imperial ways.
Let India send her turbans, and Japan
Her pictured vests from that remotest isle
Seated in the antechambers of the Sun :
And let her Western sisters for a while
Remit long envy and disunion,

And take in peace
Her hand behind the buckler of her seas,
'Gainst which their wrath has splintered ; come,
    for she
Her hand ungauntlets in mild amity.

Victoria ! Queen, whose name is victory,
Whose woman's nature sorteth best with peace,
Bid thou the cloud of war to cease
Which ever round thy wide-girt empery
Fumes, like to smoke about a burning brand,
Telling the energies which keep within
The light unquenched, as England's light shall be ;
And let this day hear only peaceful din.
For, queenly woman, thou art more than woman ;
Thy name the often-struck barbarian shuns :
Thou art the fear of England to her foemen,
The love of England to her sons.
And this thy glorious day is England's ; who
Can separate the two ?
She joys thy joys and weeps thy tears,
And she is one with all thy moods ;
Thy story is the tale of England's years,
And big with all her ills, and all her stately goods.
Now unto thee
The plenitude of the glories thou didst sow
Is garnered up in prosperous memory ;
And, for the perfect evening of thy day,
An untumultuous bliss, serenely gay,
Sweetened with silence of the after-glow.

THE VICTORIAN ODE

Nor does the joyous shout
Which all our lips give out
Jar on that quietude ; more than may do
A radiant childish crew,
With well-accordant discord fretting the soft hour,
Whose hair is yellowed by the sinking blaze
Over a low-mouthed sea. Exult, yet be not
    twirled,
England, by gusts of mere
Blind and insensate lightness ; neither fear
The vastness of thy shadow on the world.
If in the East
Still strains against its leash the unglutted beast
Of War ; if yet the cannon's lip be warm ;
Thou, whom these portents warn but not alarm,
Feastest, but with thy hand upon the sword,
As fits a warrior race :
Not like the Saxon fools of olden days,
With the mead dripping from the hairy mouth,
While all the South
Filled with the shaven faces of the Norman horde.

The NINETEENTH CENTURY

AS, fore-announced by threat of flame and smoke,
  Out of the night's lair broke
    The sun among the startled stars, whose blood
Looses its slow bright flood
Beneath the radiant onset of the sun ;
So crouches he anon,
With nostrils breathing threat of smoke and flame,
Back to the lairing night wherefrom he came.

Say, who is she,
With cloudy battle smoking round her feet,
That goes out through the exit-doors of death ;
And at the alternate limit of her path,
Where first her nascent footsteps troubled day,
Forgotten turmoil curls itself away ?
Who is she that rose
Tumultuous, and in tumult goes ?

This is she
That rose 'midst dust of a down-tumbled world,
And dies with rumour on the air
Of preparation
For a more ample devastation,
And death of ancient fairness no more fair.
First when she knew the day,
The holy poets sung her on her way :
The high, clear band that takes
Its name from heaven-acquainted mountain-lakes ;

And he
That like a star set in Italian sea ;
And he that mangled by the jaws of our
Fierce London, from all frets
Lies balmed in Roman violets ;
And other names of power,
Too recent but for worship and regret,
On whom the tears lie wet.

But not to these
She gave her heart ; her heart she gave
To the blind worm that bores the mold,
Bloodless, pertinacious, cold,
Unweeting what itself upturns,
The seer and prophet of the grave.
It reared its head from off the earth
(Which gives it life and gave it birth)
And placed upon its eyeless head a crown,
Thereon a name writ new,
' Science,' erstwhile with ampler meanings known ;
And all the peoples in their turns
Before the blind worm bowed them down.
Yet, crowned beyond its due,
Working dull way by obdurate, slow degrees,
It is a thing of sightless prophecies ;
And glories, past its own conceit,
Wait to complete
Its travail, when the mounded time is meet.
Nor measured, fit renown,
When that hour paces forth,
Shall overlook those workers of the North

And West, those patient Darwins who forthdrew
From humble dust what truth they knew,
And greater than they knew, not knowing all they
    knew.
Yet was their knowledge in its scope a Might,
Strong and true souls to measure of their sight.
Behold the broad globe in their hands comprest,
As a boy kneads a pellet, till the East
Looks in the eyes o' the West ;
And as guest whispers guest
That counters him at feast,
The Northern mouth
Leans to the attent ear of the blended South.
The fur-skinned garb justling the Northern Bear
Crosses the threshold where,
With linen wisp girt on,
Drowses the next-door neighbour of the sun.
Such their laborious worth
To change the old face of the wonted earth.

Nor were they all o' the dust ; as witness may
Davy and Faraday ;
And they
Who clomb the cars
And learned to rein the chariots of the stars ;
Or who in night's dark waters dipt their hands
To sift the hid gold from its sands ;
And theirs the greatest gift, who drew to light
By their sciential might,
The secret ladder, wherethrough all things climb
Upward from the primeval slime.

148

Nor less we praise
Him that with burnished tube betrays
The multitudinous diminutive
Recessed in virtual night
Below the surface-seas of sight ;
Him whose enchanted windows give
Upon the populated ways
Where the shy universes live
Ambushed beyond the unapprehending gaze :
The dusted anther's globe of spiky stars ;
The beetle flashing in his minute mail
Of green and golden scale ;
And every water-drop a-sting with writhing wars.
The unnoted green scale cleaving to the moist earth's
    face
Behold disclosed a conjugal embrace,
And womb—
Submitting to the tomb—
That sprouts its lusty issue :* everywhere conjoins
Either glad sex, and from unguessed-at loins
Breeds in an opulent ease
The liberal earth's increase ;
Such Valentine's sweet unsurmisèd diocese.
Nor, dying Lady, of the sons
Whom proudly owns
Thy valedictory and difficult breath,
The least are they who followed Death
Into his obscure fastnesses,
Tracked to her secret lair Disease—

---

* The prothallus of the fern, for example, which contains in itself the
two sexes, and decays as the young fern sprouts from it.

Under the candid-seeming and confederate Day
Venoming the air's pure lips to kiss and to betray ;
Who foiled the ancient Tyrant's grey design
Unfathomed long, and brake his dusty toils,
Spoiling him of his spoils,
And man, the loud dull fly, loosed from his woven
    line.
Such triumph theirs who at the destined term
Descried the arrow flying in the day—
The age-long hidden Germ—
And threw their prescient shield before its deadly
    way.

Thou, spacious Century !
Hast seen the Western knee
Set on the Asian neck,
The dusky Africa
Kneel to imperial Europe's beck ;
The West for her permitted while didst see
Stand mistress-wise and tutelar
To the grey nations dreaming on their days afar,
From old forgotten war
Folding hands whence has slid disusèd rule ;
The while, unprescient, in her regent school
She shapes the ample days and things to be,
And large new empery.
Thence Asia shall be brought to bed
Of dominations yet undreamed ;
Narrow-eyed Egypt lift again the head
Whereon the far-seen crown Nilotic gleamed.
Thou'st seen the Saxon horde whose veins run brine,

Spawned of the salt wave, wet with the salt breeze,
Their sails combine,
Lash their bold prows together, and turn swords
Against the world's knit hordes ;
The whelps repeat the lioness' roar athwart the
     windy seas.

Yet let it grieve, grey Dame,
Thy passing spirit, God wot,
Thou wast half-hearted, wishing peace, but not
The means of it. The avaricious flame
Thou'st fanned, which thou should'st tame :
Cluck'dst thy wide brood beneath thy mothering
     plumes,
And coo'dst them from their fumes,
Stretched necks provocative, and throats
Ruffled with challenging notes ;
Yet all didst mar,
Flattering the too-much-pampered Boy of War :
Whence the far-jetting engine, and the globe
In labour with her iron progeny,—
Infernal litter of sudden-whelpèd deaths,
Vomiting venomous breaths ;
The growl as of long surf that draweth back
Half a beach in its rattling track,
When like a tiger-cat
The angry rifle spat
Its fury in the opposing foeman's eyes ;—
These are thy consummating victories,
For this hast thou been troubled to be wise !

And now what child is this upon thy lap,
Born in the red glow of relighted war ?
That draws Bellona's pap,
—Fierce foster-mother !—does already stare
With mimicked dark regard
And copied threat of brow whose trick it took from
    her :
Young Century, born to hear
The cannon talking at its infant ear—
The Twentieth of Time's loins, since that
Which in the quiet snows of Bethlehem he begat.
Ah ! with forthbringing such and so ill-starred,
After the day of blood and night of fate,
Shall it survive with brow no longer marred,
Lip no more wry with hate ;
With all thou hadst of good,
But from its blood
Washed thine hereditary ill,
Yet thy child still ?

PEACE

ON THE TREATY IN SOUTH AFRICA IN 1902

PEACE :—as a dawn that flares
Within the brazier of the barrèd East,
Kindling the ruinous walls of storm surceased
To rent and roughened glares,
After such night when lateral wind and rain
Torment the to-and-fro perplexèd trees
With thwart encounter ; which, of fixture strong,
Take only strength from the endurèd pain :
And throat by throat begin
The birds to make adventure of sweet din,
Till all the forest prosper into song :—
    Peace, even such a peace,
(O be my words an auspice !) dawns again
Upon our England, from her lethargies
Healed by that baptism of *her* cleansing pain.

Ended, the long endeavour of the land :
Ended, the set of manhood towards the sand
Of thirsty death ; and their more deadly death,
Who brought back only what they fain had lost,
No more worth-breathing breath,—
Gone the laborious and use-working hand.
Ended, the patient drip of women's tears,
Which joined the patient drip of faithful blood
To make of blood and water the sore flood
That pays our conquest's costliest cost.
This day, if fate dispose,
Shall make firm friends from firm and firm-met foes.

And now, Lord, since Thou hast upon hell's floor
Bound, like a snoring sea, the blood-drowsed bulk
    of War,
Shall we not cry, on recognising knees,
This is Thy peace ?

If, England, it be but to lay
The heavy head down, the old heavy way ;
Having a space awakened and been bold
To break from them that had thee in the snare,—
Resume the arms of thy false Dalila, Gold,
Shameful and nowise fair :
Forget thy sons who have lain down in bed
With Dingaan and old dynasties, nor heed
The ants that build their empires overhead ;
Forget their large in thy contracted deed,
And that thou stand'st twice-pledged to being great
For whom so many children greatly bleed,
Trusting thy greatness with their deaths : if thou,
England, incapable of proffered fate,
See in such deaths as these
But purchased pledges of unhindered mart,
And hirelings spent that in thy ringed estate
For some space longer now
Thou mayst add gain to gain, and take thine ease,—
God has made hard thy heart ;
Thou hast but bought thee respite, not surcease.
Lord, this is not Thy peace !

But wilt thou, England, stand
With vigilant heart and prescient brain ?—·

PEACE

Knowing there is no peace
Such as fools deem, of equal-balanced ease :—
That they who build the State
Must, like the builders of Jerusalem,
The trowel in their hand,
Work with the sword laid ever nigh to them.
If thou hold Honour worthy gain
At price of gold and pain ;
And all thy sail and cannon somewhat more
Than the fee'd watchers of the rich man's store.
If thou discern the thing which all these ward
Is that imperishable thing, a Name,
And that Name, England, which alone is lord
Where myriad-armèd India owns with awe
A few white faces ; uttered forth in flame
Where circling round the earth
Has English battle roared ;
Deep in mid-forest African a Law ;
That in this Name's small girth
The treasure is, thy sword and navies guard :
If thou wilt crop the specious sins of ease,
Whence still is War's increase,—
Proud flesh which asks for War, the knife of God,
Save to thyself, thyself use cautery ;
Wilt stay the war of all with all at odd,
And teach thy jarring sons
Truth innate once,—
That in the whole alone the part is blest and great.
O should this fire of war thus purge away
The inveterate stains of too-long ease,
And yield us back our Empire's clay

Into one shoreless State
Compact and hardened for its uses : these
No futile sounds of joyance are to-day :—
Lord, unrebuked we may
Call this Thy peace !

And in this day be not
Wholly forgot
They that made possible but shall not see
Our solemn jubilee.
Peace most to them who lie
Beneath unnative sky ;
In whose still hearts is dipt
Our reconciling script :
Peace ! But when shouts shall start the housetop
  bird,
Let these, that speak not, be the loudest heard !

CECIL RHODES

DIED MARCH 26, 1902

THEY that mis-said
This man yet living, praise him dead.
And I too praise, yet not the baser things
Wherewith the market and the tavern rings.
Not that high things for gold,
He held, were bought and sold,
That statecraft's means approved are by the end ;
Not for all which commands
The loud world's clapping hands,
To which cheap press and cheaper patriots bend ;
But for the dreams,
For those impossible gleams
He half made possible ; for that he was
Visioner of vision in a most sordid day :
This draws
Back to me Song long alien and astray.

In dreams what did he not,
Wider than his wide deeds? In dreams he wrought
What the old world's long livers must in act forego.
From the Zambesi to the Lìmpopo
He the many-languaged land
Took with his large compacting hand
And pressed into a nation : 'thwart the accurst
And lion-'larumed ways,
Where the lean-fingered Thirst
Wrings at the throat, and Famine strips the bone ;
A tawny land, with sun at sullen gaze,
And all above a cope of heated stone ;

157

He heard the shirted miner's rough halloo
Call up the mosquèd Cairene ; harkened clear
The Cairene's far-off summons sounding through
The sea's long noises to the Capeman's ear.

He saw the Teuton and the Saxon grip
Hands round the warded world, and bid it rock,
While they did watch its cradle. Like a ship
It swung, whileas the cabined inmates slept,
Secure their peace was kept,
Such arms of warranty about them lock.
Ophir* he saw, her long-ungazed-at gold,
Stirred from its deep
And often-centuried sleep,
Wink at the new Sun in an English hold ;
England, from Afric's swarthy loins
Drawing fecundity,
Wax to the South and North,
To East and West increase her puissant goings-
    forth,
And strike young emperies, like coins,
In her own recent effigy.
He saw the three-branched Teuton hold the sides
Of the round world, and part it as a dish
Whereof to each his wish
The amity of the full feast decides.

So large his dreams, so little come to act !
Who must call on the cannon to compact

* Rhodesia, according to some modern views.

CECIL RHODES

The hard Dutch-stubborned land,
Seditious even to such a potent hand ;
Who grasped and held his Ophir : held, no less,
The Northern ways, but never lived to see
The wing-foot messages
Dart from the Delta to the Southern Sea ;
Who, confident of gold,
A leaner on the statesman's arts
And the unmartial conquests of the marts,
Died with the sound of battle round him rolled,
And rumour of battle in all nations' hearts ;
Dying, saw his life a thing
Of large beginnings ; and for young
Hands yet untrained the harvesting,
Amid the iniquitous years if harvest sprung.

So in his death he sowed himself anew ;
Cast his intents over the grave to strike
In the left world of livers living roots,
And, banyan-like,
From his one tree raise up a wood of shoots.
The indestructible intents which drew
Their sap from him
Thus, with a purpose grim,
Into strange lands and hostile yet he threw,
That there might be
From him throughout the earth posterity :
And so did he—
Like to a smouldering fire by wind-blasts swirled—
His dying embers strew to kindle all the world.

Yet not for this I praise
The ending of his strenuous days ;
No, not alone that still
Beyond the grave stretched that imperial Will :
But that Death seems
To set the gateway wide to ampler dreams.
Yea, yet he dreams upon Matoppo hill,
The while the German and the Saxon see,
And seeing, wonder,
The spacious dreams take shape and be,
As at compulsion of his sleep thereunder.
Lo, young America at the Mother's knee,
Unlearning centuried hate,
For love's more blest extreme ;
And this is in his dream,
And sure the dream is great.
Lo, Colonies on Colonies,
The furred Canadian and the digger's shirt,
To the one Mother's skirt
Cling, in the lore of Empire to be wise ;
A hundred wheels a-turn
All to one end—that England's sons may learn
The glory of their sonship, the supreme
Worth that befits the heirs of such estate.
All these are in his dream,
And sure the dream is great.

So, to the last
A visionary vast,
The aspirant soul would have the body lie
Among the hills immovably exalt

CECIL RHODES

As he above the crowd that haste and halt,
' Upon that hill which I
Called " View of All the World " ' ; to show thereby
That still his unappeasable desires
Beneath his feet surveyed the peoples and empires.
Dreams, haply of scant worth,
Bound by our little thumb-ring of an earth ;
Yet an exalted thing
By the gross search for food and raimenting.
So in his own Matoppos, high, aloof,
The elements for roof,
Claiming his mountain kindred, and secure,
Within that sepulture
Stern like himself and unadorned,
From the loud multitude he ruled and scorned,
There let him cease from breath,—
Alone in crowded life, not lonelier in death.

OF NATURE : LAUD AND PLAINT

LO, here stand I and Nature, gaze to gaze,
    And I the greater. Couch thou at my feet,
    Barren of heart, and beautiful of ways,
Strong to weak purpose, fair and brute-brained beast.
I am not of thy fools
Who goddess thee with impious flatteries sweet,
Stolen from the little Schools
Which cheeped when that great mouth of Rydal ceased.
A little suffer that I try
What thou art, Child, and what am I—
Thy younger, forward brother, subtle and small,
As thou art gross and of thy person great withal.

Behold, the child
With Nature needs not to be reconciled.
The babe that keeps the womb
Questions not if with love
The life, distrainèd for its uses, come ;
Nor we demand, then, of
The Nature who is in us and around us,
Whose life doth compass, feed, and bound us,
What prompteth her to bless
With gifts, unknown for gifts, our innocent thankless-
    ness.
Mother unguessed is she, to whom
We still are in the womb.
Then comes the incidental day
When our young mouth is weaned ; and from her arms
    we stray.

OF NATURE : LAUD AND PLAINT

'Tis over ; not, mistake me not,
Those divine gleams forgot
Which one with a so ampler mouth hath sung ;
Not of these sings
My weak endeavouring tongue ;
But of those simpler things
Less heavenful : the unstrained integrity
Moving most natively,
As the glad customed lot
Of birthright privilege allows,
Through the domestic chambers of its Father's house ;
The virgin hills, provoking to be trod ;
The cloud, the stream, the tree,
The allowing bosom of the warm-breathed sod—
No alien and untemptable delight.
The wonder in a wondrous sight
Was wondrous simple, as our simple God—
Yet not dulled, daily, base,
But sweet and safe possession as our mother's face,
Which we knew not for sweet, but sweetly had ;
For who says—' Lo, how sweet ! ' has first said—' Lo,
    how sad ! '

This, not to be regained with utmost sighs,
This unconsidered birthright, is made void
As Edom's, and destroyed.
Grown man, we now despise
Thee, known for woman, nor too wise ;
As still the mother human
Is known for not too wise, and even woman.
We take ingrateful, for a blinded while,

Thine ignorant, sweet smile.
Yield maids their eyes unto their lovers' gaze ?—
Why, so dost thou. And is their gracious favour
Doled but to draw us on through warpèd ways,
Delays behind delays,
To tempt with scent,
And to deny the savour ?—
Ah, Lady, if that vengeance were thy bent,
Woman should 'venge thee for thy scornèd smiles :
Her ways are as thy ways,
Her wiles are as thy wiles.

No second joy ; one only first and over,
Which all life wanders from and looks back to ;
For sweet too sweet, till sweet is past recover :—
Let bitter Love and every bitter lover
Say, *Love's not bitter*, if I speak not true.
The first kiss to repeat !
The first ' Mine only Sweet ! '
Thine only sweet that sweetness, very surely,
And a sour truth thou spakest, if thou knew.
That first kiss to restore
By Nature given so frankly, taken so securely !
To knit again the broken chain ; once more
To run and be to the Sun's bosom caught ;
Over life's bended brows prevail
With laughters of the insolent nightingale,
Jocund of heart in darkness ; to be taught
Once more the daisy's tale,
And hear each sun-smote buttercup clang bold,
A beaten gong of gold ;

OF NATURE : LAUD AND PLAINT

To call delaying Phœbus up with chanticleer ;
Once more, once more to see the Dawn unfold
Her rosy bosom to the married Sun ;
Fulfilled with his delight,
Perfected in sweet fear—
Sweet fear, that trembles for sweet joy begun
As slowly drops the swathing night,
And all her barèd beauty lies warm-kissed and won !

No extreme rites of penitence avail
To lighten thee of knowledge, to impart
Once more the language of the daisy's tale,
And that doctorial Art
Of knowing-not to thine oblivious heart !
Of all the vain
Words of man's mouth, there are no words so vain
As ' once more ' and ' again ' !
Hope not of Nature ; she nor gives nor teaches ;
She suffers thee to take
But what thine own hand reaches,
And can itself make sovereign for thine ache.
Ah, hope not her to heal
The ills she cannot feel,
Or dry with many-businessed hand the tear
Which never yet was weak
In her unfretted eyes, on her uncarkèd cheek.

O heart of Nature ! did man ever hear
Thy yearned-for word, supposèd dear ?—
His pleading voice returns to him alone ;
He hears none other tone.

No, no ;
Take back, O poets, your praises little-wise,
Nor fool weak hearts to their unshunned distress,
Who deem that even after your device
They shall lie down in Nature's holiness :
For it was never so ;
She has no hands to bless.
Her pontiff thou ; she looks to thee,
O man ; she has no use, nor asks not, for thy knee,
Which but bewilders her,
Poor child ; nor seeks thy fealty,
And those divinities thou wouldst confer.
If thou wouldst bend in prayer,
Arise, pass forth ; thou must look otherwhere.
Thy travail all is null ;
This Nature fair,
This gate is closèd, this Gate Beautiful,—
No man shall go in there,
Since the Lord God did pass through it ;
'Tis sealed unto the King,
The King Himself shall sit
Therein, with them that are His following.
Go, leave thy labour null ;
Ponder this thing.

Lady divine !
That giv'st to men good wine,
And yet the best thou hast
And nectarous, keepest to the last,
And bring'st not forth before the Master's sign :—
How few there be thereof that ever taste,

OF NATURE : LAUD AND PLAINT

Quaffing in brutish haste,
Without distinction of thy great repast !
For ah, this Lady I have much miscalled ;
Nor fault in her, but in thy wooing is ;
And her allowèd lovers that are installed,
Find her right frank of her sweet heart, y-wis.
Then if thy wooing thou aright wouldst 'gin,
Lo here the door ; strait and rough-shapen 'tis,
And scant they be that ever here make stays,
But do the lintel miss,
In dust of these blind days.
Knock, tarry thou, and knock,
Although it seem but rock :
Here is the door where thou must enter in
To heart of Nature and of Woman too,
And olden things made new.
Stand at the door and knock ;
For it unlocked
Shall all locked things unlock,
And win but here, thou shalt to all things win,
And thou no more be mocked.
For know, this Lady Nature thou hast left,
Of whom thou fear'st thee reft,
This Lady is God's Daughter, and she lends
Her hand but to His friends,
But to her Father's friends the hand which thou
        wouldst win ;
Then enter in,
And here is that which shall for all make mends.

SONNETS

AD AMICAM

I

DEAR Dove, that bear'st to my sole-labouring ark
The olive-branch of so long wishèd rest,
When the white solace glimmers through my dark
Of nearing wings, what comfort in my breast!
Oh, may that doubted day not come, not come,
When you shall fail, my heavenly messenger,
And drift into the distance and the doom
Of all my impermissible things that were!
Rather than so, now make the sad farewell,
Which yet may be with not too-painèd pain,
Lest I again the acquainted tale should tell
Of sharpest loss that pays for shortest gain.
Ah, if my heart should hear no white wings thrill
Against its waiting window, open still!

SONNETS

II*

WHEN from the blossoms of the noiseful day
Unto the hive of sleep and hushèd gloom
Throng the dim-wingèd dreams—what dreams are they
That with the wildest honey hover home ?
Oh, they that have from many thousand thoughts
Stolen the strange sweet of ever-blossomy you,
A thousand fancies in fair-coloured knots
Which you are inexhausted meadow to.
Ah, what sharp heathery honey, quick with pain,
Do they bring home ! It holds the night awake
To hear their lovely murmur in my brain ;
And Sleep's wings have a trouble for your sake.
Day and you dawn together : for at end
With the first light breaks the first thought—
'My friend ! '

*Both in its theme and in its imagery this sonnet was written as a variation of Mrs. Meynell's verses 'At Night.'

AD AMICAM

III

O FRIEND, who mak'st that mis-spent word of
' friend '
Sweet as the low note that a summer dove
Fondles in her warm throat ! And shall it end,
Because so swift on friend and friend broke love ?
Lo, when all words to honour thee are spent,
And flung a bold stave to the old bald Time
Telling him that he is too insolent
Who thinks to rase thee from my heart or rhyme ;
Whereof to one because thou life hast given,
The other yet shall give a life to thee,
Such as to gain, the prowest swords have striven,
And compassed weaker immortality :
These spent, my heart not stinteth in her breast
Her sweet ' Friend ! friend ! '—one note, and
loves it best.

SONNETS

IV

NO, no, it cannot be, it cannot be,
  Because this love of close-affinèd friends
  In its sweet sudden ambush toilèd me
So swift, that therefore all as swift it ends.
For swift it was, yet quiet as the birth
  Of smoothest Music in a Master's soul,
Whose mild fans lapsing as she slides to earth
  Waver in the bold arms which dare control
Her from her lineal heaven ; yea, it was still
  As the young Moon that bares her nightly breast,
And smiles to see the Babe earth suck its fill.
  O Halcyon ! was thine auspice not of rest ?
      Shall this proud verse bid after-livers see
      How friends could love for immortality ?

AD AMICAM

V

WHEN that part heavenliest of all-heavenly you
      First at my side did breathe its blossomy air,
      What lovely wilderment alarmed me through!
   On what ambrosial effluence did I fare,
And comforts Paradisal ! What gales came,
   Through ports for one divinest space ajar,
Of rankèd lilies blown into a flame
   By watered banks where walks of young Saints are !
One attent space, my trembling locks did rise
   Swayed on the wind, in planetary wheel
Of intervolving sweet societies,
   From wavèd vesture and from fledgèd heel
      Odorous aspersion trailing. Then, alone
      In her eyes' central glory, God took throne.

TO A CHILD

WHENAS my Life shall time with funeral
  tread
  The heavy death-drum of the beaten hours,
Following, sole mourner, mine own manhood dead,
 Poor forgot corse, where not a maid strows flowers ;
When I you love am no more I you love,
 But go with unsubservient feet, behold
Your dear face through changed eyes, all grim
  change prove ;—
 A new man, mockèd with misname of old ;
When shamed Love keeps his ruined lodging, elf !
 When, ceremented in mouldering memory,
Myself is hearsèd underneath myself,
 And I am but the monument of me :—
   O to that tomb be tender then, which bears
   Only the name of him it sepulchres !

HERMES

SOOTHSAY. Behold, with rod twy-serpented,
Hermes the prophet, twining in one power
The woman with the man. Upon his head
The cloudy cap, wherewith he hath in dower
The cloud's own virtue—change and counterchange,
To show in light, and to withdraw in pall,
As mortal eyes best bear. His lineage strange
From Zeus, Truth's sire, and maiden May—the all
Illusive Nature. His fledged feet declare
That 'tis the nether self transdeified,
And the thrice-furnaced passions, which do bear
The poet Olympusward. In him allied
Both parents clasp ; and from the womb of Nature
Stern Truth takes flesh in shows of lovely feature.

HOUSE OF BONDAGE

I

WHEN I perceive Love's heavenly reaping still
Regard perforce the clouds' vicissitude,
That the fixed spirit loves not when it will,
But craves its seasons of the flawful blood;
When I perceive that the high poet doth
Oft voiceless stray beneath the uninfluent stars,
That even Urania of her kiss is loth,
And Song's brave wings fret on their sensual bars;
When I perceive the fullest-sailèd sprite
Lag at most need upon the lethèd seas,
The provident captainship oft voided quite,
And lamèd lie deep-draughted argosies;
    I scorn myself, that put for such strange toys
    The wit of man to purposes of boys.

HOUSE OF BONDAGE

II

THE spirit's ark sealed with a little clay
  Was old ere Memphis grew a memory ;*
  The hand pontifical to break away
That seal what shall surrender ? Not the sea
Which did englut great Egypt and his war,
  Nor all the desert-drownèd sepulchres.
Love's feet are stained with clay and travel-sore,
  And dusty are Song's lucent wing and hairs.
O Love, that must do courtesy to decay,
  Eat hasty bread standing with loins up-girt,
How shall this stead thy feet for their sore way ?
  Ah, Song, what brief embraces balm thy hurt !
    Had Jacob's toil full guerdon, casting his
    Twice-seven heaped years to burn in Rachel's
    kiss ?

* The Ark of the Egyptian temple was sealed with clay, which the
Pontiff-King broke when he entered the inner shrine to offer worship.

THE HEART

To my Critic who had objected to the phrase—
'The heart's burning floors.'

I

THE heart you hold too small and local thing
  Such spacious terms of edifice to bear.
  And yet, since Poesy first shook out her wing,
The mighty Love has been impalaced there ;
That has she given him as his wide demesne,
  And for his sceptre ample empery ;
Against its door to knock has Beauty been
  Content ; it has its purple canopy,
A dais for the sovereign lady spread
  Of many a lover, who the heaven would think
Too low an awning for her sacred head.
    The world, from star to sea, cast down its brink—
      Yet shall that chasm, till He Who these did
        build
      An awful Curtius make Him, yawn unfilled.

THE HEART

II

ONOTHING, in this corporal earth of man,
  That to the imminent heaven of his high soul
  Responds with colour and with shadow, can
Lack correlated greatness. If the scroll
Where thoughts lie fast in spell of hieroglyph
  Be mighty through its mighty habitants ;
If God be in His Name ; grave potence if
  The sounds unbind of hieratic chants ;
All's vast that vastness means. Nay, I affirm
  Nature is whole in her least things exprest,
Nor know we with what scope God builds the worm.
  Our towns are copied fragments from our breast ;
    And all man's Babylons strive but to impart
    The grandeurs of his Babylonian heart.

DESIDERIUM
INDESIDERATUM

O GAIN that lurk'st ungainèd in all gain !
O love we just fall short of in all love !
O height that in all heights art still above !
O beauty that dost leave all beauty pain !
Thou unpossessed that mak'st possession vain,
See these strained arms which fright the simple air,
And say what ultimate fairness holds thee, Fair !
They girdle Heaven, and girdle Heaven in vain ;
They shut, and lo ! but shut in their unrest.
Thereat a voice in me that voiceless was :—
' Whom seekest thou through the unmarged arcane,
And not discern'st to thine own bosom prest ? '
I looked. My claspèd arms athwart my breast
Framed the august embraces of the Cross.

LOVE'S VARLETS

LOVE, he is nearer (though the moralist
 Of rule and line cry shame on me), more near
 To thee and to the heart of thee, be't wist,
Who sins against thee even for the dear
Lack that he hath of thee ; than who, chill-wrapt
 In thy light-thought-on customed livery,
Keeps all thy laws with formal service apt,
 Save that great law to tremble and to be
Shook to his heart-strings if there do but pass
 The rumour of thy pinions. Such one is
Thy varlet, guerdoned with the daily mass
 That feed on thy remainder-meats of bliss.
  More hath he of thy bosom, whose slips of
   grace
  Fell through despair of thy close-gracious face.

NON PAX—EXPECTATIO

HUSH! 'tis the gap between two lightnings. Room
Is none for peace in this thou callest peace,
This breathing-while wherein the breathings
cease.
The pulses sicken, hearkening through the gloom.
Afar the thunders of a coming doom
Ramp on the cowering winds. Lo! at the dread,
Thy heart's tomb yawns and renders up its dead,—
The hopes 'gainst hope embalmèd in its womb.

Canst thou endure, if the pent flood o'erflows?
Who is estated heir to constancy?
Behold, I hardly know if I outlast
The minute underneath whose heel I lie ;
Yet I endure, have stayed the minute passed,
Perchance may stay the next. Who knows, who knows?

NOT EVEN IN DREAM

THIS love is crueller than the other love :
    We had the Dreams for Tryst, we other pair ;
    But here there is no *we* ;—not anywhere
Returning breaths of sighs about me move.
No wings, even of the stuff which fancy wove,
    Perturb Sleep's air with a responsive flight
When mine sweep into dreams. My soul in fright
    Circles as round its widowed nest a dove.

One shadow but usurps another's place :
    And, though this shadow more enthralling is,
Alas, it hath no lips at all to miss !
    I have not even that former poignant bliss,
That haunting sweetness, that forlorn sad trace,
    The phantom memory of a vanished kiss.

MISCELLANEOUS POEMS

A HOLLOW WOOD

THIS is the mansion built for me
  By the sweating centuries ;
  Roofed with intertwinèd tree,
Woofed with green for my princelier ease.
Here I lie with my world about me,
Shadowed off from the world without me,
Even as my thoughts embosom me
From wayside humanity.
And here can only enter who
Delight me—the unpricèd few.
Come you in, and make you cheer,
It draweth toward my banquet-time.
Would you win to my universe,
Your thought must turn in the wards of rhyme.
Loose the chain of linkèd verse,
Stoop your knowledge, and enter here !

Here cushioned ivies you invite
To fall to with appetite.
What for my viands ?—Dainty thoughts.
What for my brows ?—Forget-me-nots.
What for my feet ?—A bath of green.
My servers ?—Phantasies unseen.
What shall I find me for feasting dress ?—
Your white disusèd childlikeness.
What hid music will laugh to my calls ?—
An orgy of mad bird-bacchanals.
Such meat, such music, such coronals !
From the cask which the summer sets aflow

Under the roof of my raftered house,
The birds above, we below,
We carouse as they carouse.
Or have but the ear the ear within,
And you may hear, if you hold you mute,
You may hear by my amulet,
The wind-like keenness of violin,
The enamelled tone of shallow flute,
And the furry richness of clarinet.
These are the things shall make you cheer,
If you will grace my banquet-time.
Would you win to my universe,
Your thought must turn in the wards of rhyme.
Loose the chain of linkèd verse,
Stoop your knowledge, and enter here !

TO DAISIES

AH, drops of gold in whitening flame
  Burning, we know your lovely name—
  Daisies, that little children pull !
Like all weak things, over the strong
Ye do not know your power for wrong,
And much abuse your feebleness.
Weak maids, with flutter of a dress,
Increase most heavy tyrannies ;
And vengeance unto heaven cries
For multiplied injustice of dove-eyes.
Daisies, that little children pull,
As ye are weak, be merciful !
O hide your eyes ! they are to me
Beautiful insupportably.
Or be but conscious ye are fair,
And I your loveliness could bear ;
But, being fair so without art,
Ye vex the silted memories of my heart !

As a pale ghost yearning strays
With sundered gaze,
'Mid corporal presences that are
To it impalpable—such a bar
Sets you more distant than the morning-star.
Such wonder is on you and amaze,
I look and marvel if I be
Indeed the phantom, or are ye ?
The light is on your innocence
Which fell from me.

The fields ye still inhabit whence
My world-acquainted treading strays,
The country where I did commence ;
And though ye shine to me so near,
So close to gross and visible sense,
Between us lies impassable year on year.
To other time and far-off place
Belongs your beauty : silent thus,
Though to others naught you tell,
To me your ranks are rumorous
Of an ancient miracle.

Vain does my touch your petals graze,
I touch you not ; and, though ye blossom here,
Your roots are fast in alienated days.
Ye there are anchored, while Time's stream
Has swept me past them : your white ways
And infantile delights do seem
To look in on me like a face,
Dead and sweet, come back through dream,
With tears, because for old embrace
It has no arms. These hands did toy,
Children, with you when I was child,
And in each other's eyes we smiled :
Not yours, not yours the grievous-fair
Apparelling
With which you wet mine eyes ; you wear,
Ah me, the garment of the grace
I wove you when I was a boy ;
O mine, and not the year's, your stolen Spring !
And since ye wear it,

TO DAISIES

Hide your sweet selves ! I cannot bear it.
For, when ye break the cloven earth
With your young laughter and endearment,
No blossomy carillon 'tis of mirth
To me ; I see my slaughtered joy
Bursting its cerement.

TO THE SINKING SUN

HOW graciously thou wear'st the yoke
　　Of use that does not fail !
　The grasses, like an anchored smoke,
　　Ride in the bending gale ;
This knoll is snowed with blosmy manna,
　　And fire-dropt as a seraph's mail.

Here every eve thou stretchest out
　　Untarnishable wing,
And marvellously bring'st about
　　Newly an olden thing ;
Nor ever through like-ordered heaven
　　Moves largely thy grave progressing.

Here every eve thou goest down
　　Behind the self-same hill,
Nor ever twice alike go'st down
　　Behind the self-same hill ;
Nor like-ways is one flame-sopped flower
　　Possessed with glory past its will.

Not twice alike ! I am not blind,
　　My sight is live to see ;
And yet I do complain of thy
　　Weary variety.
O Sun ! I ask thee less or more,
　　Change not at all, or utterly !

TO THE SINKING SUN

O give me unprevisioned new,
   Or give to change reprieve !
For new in me is olden too,
   That I for sameness grieve.
O flowers ! O grasses ! be but once
   The grass and flower of yester-eve !

Wonder and sadness are the lot
   Of change : thou yield'st mine eyes
Grief of vicissitude, but not
   Its penetrant surprise.
Immutability mutable
   Burthens my spirit and the skies.

O altered joy, all joyed of yore,
   Plodding in unconned ways !
O grief grieved out, and yet once more
   A dull, new, staled amaze !
I dream, and all was dreamed before,
   Or dream I so ? the dreamer says.

A MAY BURDEN

THROUGH meadow-ways as I did tread,
The corn grew in great lustihead,
And hey! the beeches burgeonèd.
    By Goddès fay, by Goddès fay!
It is the month, the jolly month,
It is the jolly month of May.

God ripe the wines and corn, I say,
And wenches for the marriage-day,
And boys to teach love's comely play.
    By Goddès fay, by Goddès fay!
It is the month, the jolly month,
It is the jolly month of May.

As I went down by lane and lea,
The daisies reddened so, pardie!
' Blushets! ' I said, ' I well do see,
    By Goddès fay, by Goddès fay!
The thing ye think of in this month,
Heigho! this jolly month of May.'

As down I went by rye and oats,
The blossoms smelt of kisses ; throats
Of birds turned kisses into notes ;
    By Goddès fay, by Goddès fay!
The kiss it is a growing flower,
I trow, this jolly month of May!

A MAY BURDEN

God send a mouth to every kiss,
Seeing the blossom of this bliss
By gathering doth grow, certes !
    By Goddès fay, by Goddès fay !
Thy brow-garland pushed all aslant
Tells—but I tell not, wanton May !

The first two stanzas are from a French original—I have
forgotten what.

JULY FUGITIVE

CAN you tell me where has hid her
    Pretty Maid July ?
    I would swear one day ago
    She passed by,
I would swear that I do know
    The blue bliss of her eye :
' Tarry, maid, maid,' I bid her ;
    But she hastened by.
Do you know where she has hid her,
    Maid July ?

Yet in truth it needs must be
    The flight of her is old ;
Yet in truth it needs must be,
    For her nest, the earth, is cold.
No more in the poolèd Even
    Wade her rosy feet,
Dawn-flakes no more plash from them
    To poppies 'mid the wheat.
She has muddied the day's oozes
    With her petulant feet ;
Scared the clouds that floated,
    As sea-birds they were,
Slow on the cœrule
    Lulls of the air,
Lulled on the luminous
    Levels of air :
She has chidden in a pet
    All her stars from her .

198

JULY FUGITIVE

Now they wander loose and sigh
    Through the turbid blue,
Now they wander, weep, and cry—
    Yea, and I too—
' Where are you, sweet July,
    Where are you ? '

Who hath beheld her footprints,
    Or the pathway she goes ?
Tell me, wind, tell me, wheat,
    Which of you knows ?
Sleeps she swathed in the flushed Arctic
    Night of the rose ?
Or lie her limbs like Alp-glow
    On the lily's snows ?
Gales, that are all-visitant,
    Find the runaway ;
And for him who findeth her
    (I do charge you say)
I will throw largesse of broom
    Of this summer's mintage,
I will broach a honey-bag
    Of the bee's best vintage.
Breezes, wheat, flowers sweet,
    None of them knows !
How then shall we lure her back
    From the way she goes ?
For it were a shameful thing,
    Saw we not this comer
Ere Autumn camp upon the fields
    Red with rout of Summer.

When the bird quits the cage,
   We set the cage outside,
With seed and with water,
   And the door wide,
Haply we may win it so
   Back to abide.
Hang her cage of Earth out
   O'er Heaven's sunward wall,
Its four gates open, winds in watch
   By reinèd cars at all ;
Relume in hanging hedgerows
   The rain-quenched blossom,
And roses sob their tears out
   On the gale's warm heaving bosom ;
Shake the lilies till their scent
   Over-drip their rims ;
That our runaway may see
   We do know her whims :
Sleek the tumbled waters out
   For her travelled limbs ;
Strew and smooth blue night thereon :
   There will—O not doubt her !—
The lovely sleepy lady lie,
   With all her stars about her !

FIELD-FLOWER
A PHANTASY

GOD took a fit of Paradise-wind,
  A slip of cœrule weather,
  A thought as simple as Himself,
And ravelled them together.
Unto His eyes He held it there,
To teach it gazing debonair
  With memory of what, perdie,
A God's young innocences were.
His fingers pushed it through the sod—
It came up redolent of God,
Garrulous of the eyes of God
  To all the breezes near it ;
Musical of the mouth of God
  To all had ears to hear it ;
Mystical with the mirth of God,
  That glow-like did ensphere it.
     And—' Babble ! babble ! babble ! ' said ;
     ' I'll tell the whole world one day ! '
     There was no blossom half so glad,
     Since sun of Christ's first Sunday.

A poet took a flaw of pain,
  A hap of skiey pleasure,
A thought had in his cradle lain,
  And mingled them in measure.
That chrism he laid upon his eyes,
And lips, and heart, for euphrasies,
  That he might see, feel, sing, perdie,

The simple things that are the wise.
Beside the flower he held his ways,
And leaned him to it gaze for gaze—
He took its meaning, gaze for gaze,
  As baby looks on baby ;
Its meaning passed into his gaze,
  Native as meaning may be ;
He rose with all his shining gaze
  As children's eyes at play be.
     And—' Babble ! babble ! babble ! ' said ;
     ' I'll tell the whole world one day ! '
    There was no poet half so glad,
     Since man grew God that Sunday.

TO A SNOWFLAKE

WHAT heart could have thought you ?—
　　Past our devisal
　　　　(O filigree petal !)
Fashioned so purely,
Fragilely, surely,
From what Paradisal
Imagineless metal,
Too costly for cost ?
Who hammered you, wrought you,
From argentine vapour ?—
' God was my shaper.
Passing surmisal,
He hammered, He wrought me,
From curled silver vapour,
To lust of His mind :—
Thou could'st not have thought me !
So purely, so palely,
Tinily, surely,
Mightily, frailly,
Insculped and embossed,
With His hammer of wind,
And His graver of frost.'

A QUESTION

O BIRD with heart of wassail,
   That toss the Bacchic branch,
   And slip your shaken music,
An elfin avalanche ;

Come tell me, O tell me,
   My poet of the blue !
What's *your* thought of me, Sweet ?—
Here's *my* thought of you.

A small thing, a wee thing,
   A brown fleck of naught ;
With winging and singing
   That who could have thought ?

A small thing, a wee thing,
   A brown amaze withal,
That fly a pitch more azure
   Because you're so small.

Bird, I'm a small thing—
   My angel descries ;
With winging and singing
   That who could surmise ?

Ah, small things, ah, wee things,
   Are the poets all,
Whose tour's the more azure
   Because they're so small.

A QUESTION

The angels hang watching
    The tiny men-things :—
' The dear speck of flesh, see,
    With such daring wings !

' Come, tell us, O tell us,
    Thou strange mortality !
What 's *thy* thought of us, Dear ?—
    Here 's *our* thought of thee.'

' Alack ! you tall angels,
    I can't think so high !
I can't think what it feels like
    Not to be I.'

Come tell me, O tell me,
    My poet of the blue !
What 's *your* thought of me, Sweet ?—
    Here 's *my* thought of you.

THE CLOUD'S SWAN-SONG

THERE is a parable in the pathless cloud,
There's prophecy in heaven,—they did not lie,
The Chaldee shepherds,—sealèd from the proud,
To cheer the weighted heart that mates the seeing eye.

A lonely man, oppressed with lonely ills,
And all the glory fallen from my song,
Here do I walk among the windy hills ;
The wind and I keep both one monotoning tongue.

Like grey clouds one by one my songs upsoar
Over my soul's cold peaks ; and one by one
They loose their little rain, and are no more ;
And whether well or ill, to tell me there is none.

For 'tis an alien tongue, of alien things,
From all men's care, how miserably apart !
Even my friends say : ' Of what is this he sings ? '
And barren is my song, and barren is my heart.

For who can work, unwitting his work's worth ?
Better, meseems, to know the work for naught,
Turn my sick course back to the kindly earth,
And leave to ampler plumes the jetting tops of thought.

And visitations that do often use
Remote, unhappy, inauspicious sense
Of doom, and poets widowed of their muse,
And what dark 'gan, dark ended, in me did commence.

THE CLOUD'S SWAN-SONG

I thought of spirit wronged by mortal ills,
And my flesh rotting on my fate's dull stake ;
And how self-scornèd they the bounty fills
Of others, and the bread, even of their dearest, take.

I thought of Keats, that died in perfect time,
In predecease of his just-sickening song ;
Of him that set, wrapt in his radiant rhyme,
Sunlike in sea. Life longer had been life too long.

But I, exanimate of quick Poesy,—
O then no more but even a soulless corse !
Nay, my Delight dies not ; 'tis I should be
Her dead, a stringless harp on which she had no force.

Of my wild lot I thought ; from place to place,
Apollo's song-bowed Scythian, I go on ;
Making in all my home, with pliant ways,
But, provident of change, putting forth root in none.

Now, with starved brain, sick body, patience galled
With fardels even to wincing ; from fair sky
Fell sudden little rain, scarce to be called
A shower, which of the instant was gone wholly by.

What cloud thus died I saw not ; heaven was fair.
Methinks my angel plucked my locks : I bowed
My spirit, shamed ; and looking in the air :—
'Even so,' I said, ' even so, my brother the good
      Cloud ? '

It was a pilgrim of the fields of air,
Its home was allwheres the wind left it rest,
And in a little forth again did fare,
And in all places was a stranger and a guest.

It harked all breaths of heaven, and did obey
With sweet peace their uncomprehended wills ;
It knew the eyes of stars which made no stay,
And with the thunder walked upon the lonely hills.

And from the subject earth it seemed to scorn,
It drew the sustenance whereby it grew
Perfect in bosom for the married Morn,
And of his life and light full as a maid kissed new.

Its also darkness of the face withdrawn,
And the long waiting for the little light,
So long in life so little. Like a fawn
It fled with tempest breathing hard at heel of flight ;

And having known full East, did not disdain
To sit in shadow and oblivious cold,
Save what all loss doth of its loss retain,
And who hath held hath somewhat that he still must
    hold.

Right poet ! who thy rightness to approve,
Having all liberty, didst keep all measure,
And with a firmament for ranging, move
But at the heavens' uncomprehended pleasure.

THE CLOUD'S SWAN-SONG

With amplitude unchecked, how sweetly thou
Didst wear the ancient custom of the skies,
And yoke of used prescription ; and thence how
Find gay variety no licence could devise !

As we the quested beauties better wit
Of the one grove our own than forests great,
Restraint, by the delighted search of it,
Turns to right scope. For lovely moving intricate

Is put to fair devising in the curb
Of ordered limit ; and all-changeful Hermes
Is Terminus as well. Yet we perturb
Our souls for latitude, whose strength in bound and
     term is.

How far am I from heavenly liberty,
That play at policy with change and fate,
Who should my soul from foreign broils keep free,
In the fast-guarded frontiers of its single state !

Could I face firm the Is, and with To-be
Trust Heaven ; to Heaven commit the deed, and do ;
In power contained, calm in infirmity,
And fit myself to change with virtue ever new ;

Thou hadst not shamed me, cousin of the sky,
Thou wandering kinsman, that didst sweetly live
Unnoted, and unnoted sweetly die,
Weeping more gracious song than any I can weave ;

Which these gross-tissued words do sorely wrong.
Thou hast taught me on powerlessness a power ;
To make song wait on life, not life on song ;
To hold sweet not too sweet, and bread for bread
    though sour ;

By law to wander, to be strictly free.
With tears ascended from the heart's sad sea,
Ah, such a silver song to Death could I
Sing, Pain would list, forgetting Pain to be,
And Death would tarry marvelling, and forget to die !

OF MY FRIEND

THE moonlight cloud of her invisible beauty,
    Shook from the torrent glory of her soul
    In aëry spray, hangs round her ; love grows duty,
If you that angel-populous aureole
        Have the glad power to feel ;
        As all our longings kneel
To the intense and cherub-wingèd stole
Orbing a painted Saint : and through control
        Of this sweet faint
        Veil, my unguessing Saint
Celestial ministrations sheds which heal.

     *   *   *   *

Now, Friend, short sweet outsweetening sharpest woes !
    In wintry cold a little, little flame—
So much to me that little !—here I close
    This errant song. O pardon its much blame !
        Now my grey day grows bright
        A little ere the night ;
Let after-livers who may love my name,
And gauge the price I paid for dear-bought fame,
        Know that at end,
        Pain was well paid, sweet Friend,
Pain was well paid which brought me to your sight.

TO MONICA : AFTER
NINE YEARS

IN the land of flag-lilies,
  Where burst in golden clangours
  The joy-bells of the broom,
You were full of willy-nillies,
Pets, and bee-like angers :
Flaming like a dusky poppy,
  In a wrathful bloom.

You were full of sweet and sour,
Like a dish of strawberries
Set about with curd.
In your petulant foot was power,
In your wilful innocences,
Your wild and fragrant word.
O, was it you that sweetly spake,
Or I that sweetly heard ?

Yellow were the wheat-ways,
The poppies were most red ;
And all your meet and feat ways,
Your sudden bee-like snarlings,—
Ah, do you remember,
Darling of the darlings ?
Or is it but an ember,
A rusted peal of joy-bells,
Their golden buzzings dead ?

TO MONICA : AFTER NINE YEARS

Now at one, and now at two,
Swift to pout and swift to woo,
The maid I knew :
Still I see the duskèd tresses—
But the old angers, old caresses ?
Still your eyes are autumn thunders,
But where are *you*, child, you ?

This your beauty is a script
Writ with pencil brightest-dipt—
Oh, it is the fairest scroll
For a young, departed soul !—
Thus you say :
' Thrice three years ago to-day,
There was one
Shall no more beneath the sun
Darkle, fondle, featly play.
If to think on her be gloom,
Rejoice she has so rich a tomb ! '

But there 's he—
Ask thou not who it may be !—
That, until Time's boughs are bare,
Shall be unconsoled for her.

A DOUBLE NEED

(*To W*—)

AH, gone the days when for undying kindness
    I still could render you undying song !
    You yet can give, but I can give no more ;
Fate, in her extreme blindness,
Has wrought me so great wrong.
I am left poor indeed ;
Gone is my sole and amends-making store,
And I am needy with a double need.

Behold that I am like a fountained nymph,
Lacking her customed lymph,
The longing parched in stone upon her mouth,
Unwatered of its ancient plenty. She
(Remembering her irrevocable streams),
A Thirst made marble, sits perpetually
With sundered lips of still-memorial drouth.

GRIEF'S HARMONICS

AT evening, when the lank and rigid trees,
    To the mere forms of their sweet day-selves
      drying,
On heaven's blank leaf seem pressed and flattenèd ;
Or rather, to my sombre thoughts replying,
Of plumes funereal the thin effigies ;
That hour when all old dead things seem most dead,
And their death instant most and most undying,
That the flesh aches at them ; there stirred in me
The babe of an unborn calamity,
Ere its due time to be deliverèd.
Dead sorrow and sorrow unborn so blent their pain,
That which more present was were hardly said,
But both more *now* than any Now can be.
My soul like sackcloth did her body rend,
And thus with Heaven contend :—
' Let pass the chalice of this coming dread,
Or that fore-drained O bid me not re-drain ! '
So have I asked, who know my asking vain ;
Woe against woe in antiphon set over,
That grief's soul transmigrates, and lives again,
And in new pang old pang's incarnatèd.

MEMORAT MEMORIA

COME you living or dead to me, out of the silt of
the Past,
With the sweet of the piteous first, and the shame
of the shameful last ?
Come with your dear and dreadful face through the
passes of Sleep,
The terrible mask, and the face it masked—the face you
did not keep ?
You are neither two nor one—I would you were one or
two,
For your awful self is embalmed in the fragrant self I
knew :
And Above may ken, and Beneath may ken, what I mean
by these words of whirl,
But by my sleep that sleepeth not,—O Shadow of a
Girl !—
Naught here but I and my dreams shall know the secret
of this thing :—
For ever the songs I sing are sad with the songs I never
sing,
Sad are sung songs, but how more sad the songs we dare
not sing !

Ah, the ill that we do in tenderness, and the hateful
horror of love !
It has sent more souls to the unslaked Pit than it ever
will draw above.
I damned you, girl, with my pity, who had better by far
been thwart,

And drave you hard on the track to hell, because I was
    gentle of heart.
I shall have no comfort now in scent, no ease in dew, for
    this ;
I shall be afraid of daffodils, and rose-buds are amiss ;
You have made a thing of innocence as shameful as a sin,
I shall never feel a girl's soft arms without horror of the
    skin.
My child ! what was it that I sowed, that I so ill should
    reap ɾ
You have done this to me. And I, what I to you ɾ—It
    lies with Sleep.

NOCTURN

I WALK, I only,
Not I only wake;
Nothing is, this sweet night,
But doth couch and wake
For its love's sake;
Everything, this sweet night,
Couches with its mate.
For whom but for the stealthy-visitant sun
Is the naked moon
Tremulous and elate?
The heaven hath the earth
Its own and all apart;
The hushèd pool holdeth
A star to its heart.
You may think the rose sleepeth,
But though she folded is,
The wind doubts her sleeping;
Not all the rose sleeps,
But smiles in her sweet heart
For crafty bliss.
The wind lieth with the rose,
And when he stirs, she stirs in her repose:
The wind hath the rose,
And the rose her kiss.
Ah, mouth of me!
Is it then that this
Seemeth much to thee?—
I wander only.
The rose hath her kiss.

HEAVEN AND HELL

'TIS said there were no thought of hell,
　　Save hell were taught.; that there should
　　be
A Heaven for all's self-credible.
　　Not so the thing appears to me.
'Tis Heaven that lies beyond our sights,
　　And hell too possible that proves ;
For all can feel the God that smites,
　　But ah, how few the God that loves !

'CHOSE VUE'

A Metrical Caprice

UP she rose, fair daughter—well she was graced,
   As a cloud her going, stept from her chair,
   As a summer-soft cloud in her going paced,
Down dropped her riband-band, and all her waving
    hair
Shook like loosened music cadent to her waist ;—
Lapsing iike music, wavery as water,
    Slid to her waist.

ST MONICA

AT the Cross thy station keeping
    With the mournful Mother weeping,
    Thou, unto the sinless Son,
Weepest for thy sinful one.
Blood and water from His side
Gush ; in thee the streams divide :
From thine eyes the one doth start,
But the other from thy heart.

Mary, for thy sinner, see,
To her Sinless mourns with thee :
Could that Son the son not heed,
For whom two such mothers plead ?
So thy child had baptism twice,
And the whitest from thine eyes.

The floods lift up, lift up their voice,
With a many-watered noise !
Down the centuries fall those sweet
Sobbing waters to our feet,
And our laden air still keeps
Murmur of a Saint that weeps.

Teach us but, to grace our prayers,
Such divinity of tears,—
Earth should be lustrate again
With contrition of that rain :
Till celestial floods o'er-rise
The high tops of Paradise.

MARRIAGE IN TWO MOODS

I

LOVE that's loved from day to day
    Loves itself into decay :
    He that eats one daily fruit
Shrivels hunger at the root.
Daily pleasure grows a task ;
Daily smiles become a mask.
Daily growth of unpruned strength
Expands to feebleness at length.
Daily increase thronging fast
Must devour itself at last.
Daily shining, even content
Would with itself grow discontent ;
And the sun's life witnesseth
Daily dying is not death.
So Love loved from day to day
Loves itself into decay.

II

Love to daily uses wed
Shall be sweetly perfeſted.
Life by repetition grows
Unto its appointed close :
Day to day fulfils one year—
Shall not Love by Love wax dear ?
All piles by repetition rise—
Shall not then Love's edifice ?

MARRIAGE IN TWO MOODS

Shall not Love, too, learn his writ,
Like Wisdom, by repeating it?
By the oft-repeated use
All perfections gain their thews;
And so, with daily uses wed,
Love, too, shall be perfected.

ALL FLESH

I DO not need the skies'
Pomp, when I would be wise;
For pleasaunce nor to use
Heaven's champaign when I muse.
One grass-blade in its veins
Wisdom's whole flood contains:
Thereon my foundering mind
Odyssean fate can find.

O little blade, now vaunt
Thee, and be arrogant!
Tell the proud sun that he
Sweated in shaping thee;
Night, that she did unvest
Her mooned and argent breast
To suckle thee. Heaven fain
Yearned over thee in rain,
And with wide parent wing
Shadowed thee, nested thing,
Fed thee, and slaved for thy
Impotent tyranny.
Nature's broad thews bent
Meek for thy content.
Mastering littleness
Which the wise heavens confess,
The frailty which doth draw
Magnipotence to its law—
These were, O happy one, these
Thy laughing puissances!

ALL FLESH

Be confident of thought,
Seeing that thou art naught ;
And be thy pride thou'rt all
Delectably safe and small.
Epitomized in thee
Was the mystery
Which shakes the spheres conjoint—
God focussed to a point.

All thy fine mouths shout
Scorn upon dull-eyed doubt.
Impenetrable fool
Is he thou canst not school
To the humility
By which the angels see !
Unfathomably framed
Sister, I am not shamed
Before the cherubin
To vaunt my flesh thy kin.
My one hand thine, and one
Imprisoned in God's own,
I am as God ; alas,
And such a god of grass !
A little root clay-caught,
A wind, a flame, a thought,
Inestimably naught !

THE KINGDOM OF GOD

' In no Strange Land '

O WORLD invisible, we view thee,
 O world intangible, we touch thee,
 O world unknowable, we know thee,
Inapprehensible, we clutch thee !

Does the fish soar to find the ocean,
The eagle plunge to find the air—
That we ask of the stars in motion
If they have rumour of thee there ?

Not where the wheeling systems darken,
And our benumbed conceiving soars !—
The drift of pinions, would we hearken,
Beats at our own clay-shuttered doors.

The angels keep their ancient places ;—
Turn but a stone, and start a wing !
'Tis ye, 'tis your estrangèd faces,
That miss the many-splendoured thing.

But (when so sad thou canst not sadder)
Cry ;—and upon thy so sore loss
Shall shine the traffic of Jacob's ladder
Pitched betwixt Heaven and Charing Cross.

THE KINGDOM OF GOD

Yea, in the night, my Soul, my daughter,
Cry,—clinging Heaven by the hems;
And lo, Christ walking on the water
Not of Gennesareth, but Thames!

[THIS POEM (found among his papers when he died) Francis Thompson
might yet have worked upon to remove, here a defective rhyme, there an
unexpected elision. But no altered mind would he have brought to the
purport of it;—the prevision of 'Heaven in Earth and God in Man,'
pervading his earlier published verse, is here accented by poignantly
local and personal allusion. For in these triumphing stanzas he held in
retrospect those days and nights of human dereliction he spent beside
London's River, and in the shadow—but all radiance to him—of
Charing Cross.]

THE SINGER SAITH OF
HIS SONG

THE touches of man's modern speech
    Perplex her unacquainted tongue ;
    There seems through all her songs a sound
Of falling tears. She is not young.

Within her eyes' profound arcane
    Resides the glory of her dreams ;
Behind her secret cloud of hair.
    She sees the Is beyond the Seems.

Her heart sole-towered in her steep spirit,
    Somewhat sweet is she, somewhat wan ;
And she sings the songs of Sion
    By the streams of Babylon.